ABOUT THE AUTHORS

After leaving Philpstoun in 1956 for London, Barbara (t. married Liverpudlian Ken Pattullo. Three children and five l she trained as a maths teacher, eventually becoming Head o1 ... ... a Girls' Senior School. Despite various attempts to retire, she still works part-time. Barbara and Ken now live in location six, just outside London.

Their daughter Marie, meanwhile, qualified as a solicitor in London but now lives and works in Brussels. She is inordinately proud (and relieved), however, to have been born in Scotland (location three – see above).

1949 Gala Day, Margaret Philbin processing through The Rows,
(photograph courtesy K Philbin)

Hail Philpstoun's Queen . . .

and other tales from the shale

BARBARA AND MARIE PATTULLO

Luath Press Limited

EDINBURGH

www.luath.co.uk

First Published 2004

Barbara and Marie Pattullo have asserted their rights under the Copyright, Designs and Patents Act 1988 to be identified as the authors of this work.

The paper used in this book is acid-free, neutral-sized and recyclable. It is made from low chlorine pulps produced in a low energy, low emission manner from renewable forests.

Printed and bound by
Bell & Bain Ltd., Glasgow

Typeset in 10.5 point Sabon by
S. Fairgrieve, Edinburgh, 0131 658 1763

Contents

Foreword

ON SATURDAYS AND SUNDAYS, over a twenty year period, I would often take my car the two-mile journey from the Binns to Philpstoun to collect Mary Cosgrove from her house, to bring her to a job she enjoyed as a guide for the afternoon, for visitors to the National Trust for Scotland house where my wife Kathleen and I live. Having waved her sister Hannah cheerio, Mary would regale me with stories about the Philpstoun of her youth and middle age – a time when she would cheerfully have walked, but then, as she characteristically put it, 'there are braes when there weren't braes before'.

I am not in the least astonished that Barbara and Marie Pattullo should write that the Cosgrove sisters were the inspiration for *Hail Philpstoun's Queen and other tales from the shale*.

Mary Cosgrove was a fount of fascinating information about Philpstoun. I warmly applaud the authors for the skill with which they have woven into a verbal tapestry information they have gleaned from a variety of sources and, above all, for their assiduity in tracking down events and relationships which would otherwise be lost for ever.

Tam Dalyell, MP for Linlithgow

James, Barbara and Mary Savage

Preface

Take any train from Edinburgh to Glasgow and you will probably not even notice the little village of Philpstoun as it flashes past the window. It does not look so remarkable – just another council estate, one more notch in the commuter belt.

So why does it merit this book? Because like so many other villages in the area, Philpstoun made its own place in the region's history. Because the men and women who lived there, worked there, played there during the shale days deserve that their story be told, recorded before it is too late and the old village has gone forever. Because it is just plain wrong that we know more about the lifestyle of faceless politicians than that of our own great-grandparents.

This history is dedicated to our parents, and grandparents, James and Mary Savage. It is for all of their friends, fellow villagers and everyone connected with Philpstoun's shale-oil heritage. It is also for all of us, their descendants: this is our history too.

Barbara (née Savage) and Marie Pattullo, 2004

Before the Oilmen Came

TAKE THE EDINBURGH ROAD east out of Linlithgow and, just before you get to Kingscavil and the old estate of Champfleurie, turn left down the Troughstone road. Pass the farms and go over the canal and you will find yourself in a small, unassuming, relatively modern village nestling between the Union Canal and the Edinburgh-Glasgow railway. Welcome to Philpstoun.

It might not look so unusual. There's the new development, the Council estate, the playground and the village hall. So what is so interesting?

It's built on shale.

Although most of the layout of today's village is indeed the legacy of the shale industry, its origins are a good deal older. The current village straddles two latter-day estates, belonging to Pardovan and the Laird of Philpstoun.

As with many old place names, the origins of 'Philpstoun' are unclear, although most local authorities agree that it comes from Philip's 'tun', the old English for farm (or possibly 'town' but, given the lack of any such town at the time, the former is the preferred option). Whatever local pronunciation would have you believe, and despite the sign at the Kennels on the Winchburgh side of the Threemiletown and Philpstoun junction when heading towards Linlithgow and the original lease book of James Ross & Co., there is only one 'i' in Philpstoun.

Proving the nonsense of claims that the village did not exist before the coming of the shale industry, the name of Philpstoun was recorded as long ago as 1417 and there are references to the Monks of Culross having jurisdiction over the 'Barony of Philpstoun' in medieval days.

David Dundas obtained 'lands at Philpstoun in the parish of Abercorn' from his father, John Dundas of Newliston, in about 1618, thus becoming the Laird of Philpstoun. His nephew and successor, James, was MP for Linlithgowshire 1669-1674 and during this time the Dundas family of Philpstoun used a coat of arms bearing a silver lion rampant within a red bordure. The family line can be traced down through a variety of distinguished men including two Commissioners of Supply, a Procurator of the Church of Scotland and several advocates.

The Earls of Hopetoun (forebears of the Marquesses of Linlithgow) arrived in the area in 1678 when John Hope purchased the Barony of Abercorn from

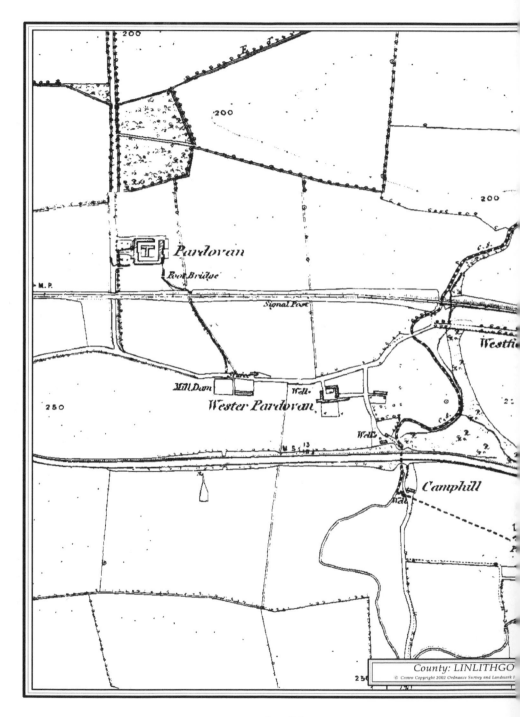

1856 Map

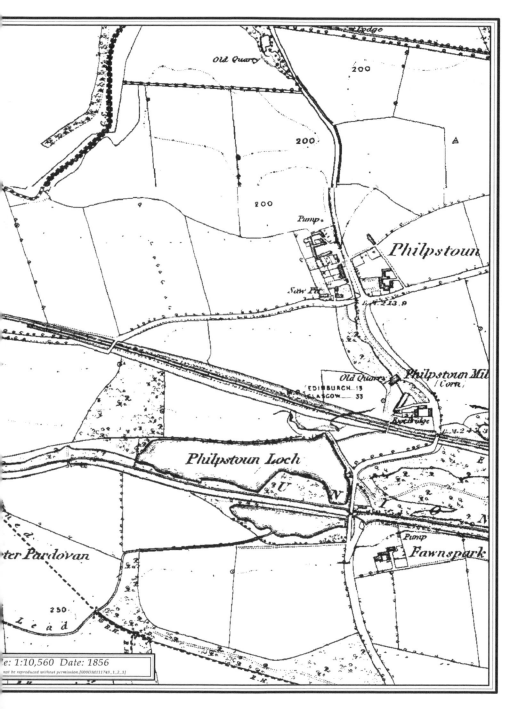

Sir Walter Seton. By the time of the Statistical Account of Scotland 1791-1799, the Philpstoun lands had already passed into the estates of Hopetoun House, residence of the Hope family from its erection between 1699 and 1702 to the present day. This connection is evidenced by 'Philpstoun House', an imposing building erected in 1676 for John Dundas which was to serve as the factor's house for the Hopetoun estate during the 19th century.

As for 'Pardovan', this may have its roots in 'Caer Pedryvan', one of the roman forts mentioned in ancient poems of the region. This theory is supported by the existence of the area under the canal bridge close to Gateside, known as 'Camphill'. Other sources suggest that it comes from the old English for 'dense grazing field'. Whichever is correct, it is sure that a 'Pardufin' was recorded as early as 1124.

The Pardovan estate, thus far older than Hopetoun, also played its part in local history. It was to the Laird of Pardovan that the Earl of Lennox surrendered after the battle of Linlithgow Bridge in 1526 and in 1570 Pardovan House was burned down by the English in revenge for the assassination of Regent Moray in Linlithgow, together with several other local properties whose owners supported Queen Mary.

That Pardovan remained an estate of consequence is evidenced by a plan of this property commissioned for the then owner, the Right Hon. Earl of Selkirk, in 1776. (The garage next to Pardovan house, originally the stable, is far older than the current house which was only built in 1896, using stone from its own quarry close to the railway).

The division of the two estates was still evident until only a few decades ago: official documents until at least the 1950s show that all land west of the Pardovan Burn – hence the centre of the modern village – was actually Wester Pardovan while the easterly part of the village was Philpstoun. That the village has taken the latter name is mainly due to the shale works being built on Philpstoun, not Pardovan, land.

The location of the village is clearly distinguishable in the 1856 Ordnance Survey map of Linlithgowshire, partly thanks to its position between the Edinburgh and Glasgow Railway and the Union Canal. Westfield (a small clutch of buildings almost opposite the Neuk) and Philpstoun Loch may have since disappeared, but the map clearly shows the farm buildings of Pardovan, Wester Pardovan, Easter Pardovan (now Fairniehill, originally spelt Ferniehill) and Fawnspark, as well as Philpstoun Mill and Philpstoun itself.

Philpstoun was a hamlet on Hopetoun land and according to *The West Lothian Courier* on 27 October 1877 it was:

a country village, and in a great measure dependent for its upholding upon its proximity to Hopetoun. There is an excellent meal mill in it, and joiner and smithy shops. Its situation is healthy and rural in the extreme. It has not increased much of late, and the number of houses will probably not exceed thirty. Though the community is not large, yet the situation of the village is not without its attractions to the student of nature, and to one who courts a calm retreat from the busy haunts of man, and the activity of trade and commerce.

'Healthy and rural' it may have been but, like so much of the locality, it was about to change beyond all recognition. The land under the village contained that precious mineral – shale – which, thanks to the uses discovered for shale-oil, was now very much in demand.

James Ross & Co. chose the village for the site of its new shale works and on 3 September 1885, the Philpstoun Oil Company started production.

CHAPTER ONE

The Shale Rush

THE GLASGOW-BORN CHEMIST James Young first made his name in academia and then in the world of chemical consultancy. While working in Manchester he conducted a number of experiments on coal oil, experiments that were so successful that they led him to set up a small oil refinery in Derbyshire in 1848 and then, in 1850, to patent his procedure for extracting, and then refining, oil from cannel coal.

Young was hardly the first person to realise that oil could be obtained from coal and shale – that had been known since at least the 17th Century. What was different in the mid 19th Century, however, was that oil was now in demand for lubrication and lighting. Better raw materials for candles were also being sought. It was this demand that was driving Young's endeavours.

James 'Paraffin' Young
(photograph courtesy of BP)

Finding coal rich enough in oil for his purposes proved difficult, until he was sent a supply of the cannel coal found at Boghead, near Bathgate. This particular cannel coal was exactly what he needed, so Young moved back to Scotland and, together with his partners, started to build the world's first commercial oil refinery at Bathgate in 1850. Given that petroleum had not even been discovered in America or the Gulf at this time, Mid and West Lothian thus became the centre of the world's oil industry.

Through the successful protection of his patents, Young was able to control the industry free from competition and his works went from strength to strength – at first. The discovery of oil-rich shale in the Broxburn and West Calder areas in 1858, the import of American petrol products (discovered in Pennsylvania in 1859) and the near exhaustion of Boghead coal supplies were threatening his survival, so Young began to diversify.

Until then no-one had been interested in paraffin, a term originally applied the wax produced as a residue from lubricating oil, or the lighter so-called burning oil. Young, however, found that there was indeed a use for this oil – lighting. After the two years he devoted to the development of lamps using this burning oil, they were so safe and so successful that the oil became known as 'paraffin' and the man would ever after be known as 'Paraffin' Young.

Young also developed other uses for the oil by-products, including candles, wax, sulphate of ammonia (an excellent fertiliser, discovered because plants grew thickly on the banks of burns by sulphate of ammonia works) and petroleum jelly.

Patents do not last forever. In 1864, Young's legal stranglehold on the industry expired and competitors sprang up almost overnight. Realising that competition from imports would only grow and that the Boghead coal supplies would not last much longer, Young decided to become part of the nascent industry that was using shale-, rather than coal-, oil. In 1865 he bought out his partners and the following year set up the Young's Paraffin Light and Mineral Oil Company with new works at Addiewell using shale from West Calder.

There was little doubt of the importance of the shale deposits in the area. To quote *Bartholomew's Gazetteer of the British Isles, 1887*:

> *Linlithgowshire is one of the richest mineral counties in Scotland, coal, shales, ironstone, freestone, limestone, &c... being very abundant. Paraffin oil is largely manufactured at Bathgate, Broxburn and Uphall.*

Shale may have given far less oil yield than Boghead coal, but it was cheap and abundant.

The Scottish shale industry was born.

Oil fever was sweeping the region, companies springing up in their dozens all over the West Lothian and Midlothian shale fields. At its peak the area boasted more than 100 different companies, some of which existed only a matter of months because, simply, entrepreneurial spirit alone is not enough to sustain a successful oil business. The result was not just new business but also new villages, and the rapid development of settlements like the Calders, Broxburn and Pumpherston.

Before the arrival of the shale industry, Linlithgowshire was almost totally rural. At its height, this industry employed over 10,000 men.

James Ross & Co. established the Philpstoun Oil Company in 1883. Unusual among its competitors, it was a private partnership and not a limited company. On 18 and 20 December 1884, the Earl of Hopetoun signed the 'Philpstoun

Lease' with Ross for 'coal oil, shale, ironstone, limestone and fireclay lying in the Estate of Hopetoun north and south of Edinburgh and Glasgow Railway with power to take possession of Philpstoun Loch'.

The lease was to run for 38 years from Lammas (1 August) 1884, with possible breaks every five years, and was the first of many mineral leases that Ross would take from Hopetoun over the years. For example, on 17 March 1885 Ross took a further lease for 'shale under Edinburgh and Bathgate Railway', in 1890 for 'shale in area of ground lying to north of Linlithgow to Queensferry road' and in 1908 for 'shale in area lying to north of Edinburgh and Glasgow Railway at Craigton including road from Craigton to Whitequarries'.

By February 1885, two mines were already open producing some 200 tons of shale per day. The company then went on to build engines and the retorts designed and patented by Norman Macfarlane Henderson, manager of the Broxburn Oil Works.

The Philpstoun Oil Company produced its first oil on 3 September 1885 in works that at their height could process some 950 tons of shale per day. The company marketed its own petrol, shipped out by canal barges to be sold as 'Ross Petrol'. (Incidentally, the petrol station at the Newton claims to be one of the oldest in the country, thanks to the local grocer having acquired a petrol pump to service the Hopetoun Estate). Their marketing pointed out that the petrol was 'the best and most economical motor spirit in the market and it is home made', and it could be found in thistle-shaped pumps emblazoned simply with 'Scotch'. Examples of pumps bearing this marvellous appellation can still be seen in some places, including the Almond Valley Heritage Centre in Livingston.

The importance of Ross's operation is clear from the reports prepared by the Government inspectors. In 1896, they show that the Philpstoun Oil Co. was under the management of AH Crichton with W Gilchrist as his under-manager (literally the manager under the ground),

Scotch Petrol Pump
(photograph courtesy
The Almond Valley Heritage Centre)

employing 164 workers underground and 19 on the surface. A 1901 report by the Sanitary Inspector put the population of Philpstoun at an estimated 765 although this included the surrounding farms and original village.

In 1908, the workforce had grown to 307 underground and 29 above with Robert Crichton as manager, while by 1918 new workings had been opened with Stewart Chambers as the area manager supported by Gilchrist, William Hogg and James Henderson underground (at number 6 pit), supervising 439 men below and 56 above the ground.

James Ross & Company Philpstoun Oil Works Limited became a limited company in 1918, the certificate of incorporation (no. 10080) and Articles of Association being signed on 12 June and witnessed by Mr Crichton's faithful secretary, Helen (Nellie) Pride. It had a share capital of £200,000 divided into 200,000 shares of £1 each. The two subscribers and directors were JF Sutherland of Solsgirth, Dollar, and Robert Crichton.

A description of the oil works from January 1926 details: 352 retorts in six benches; a sulphate of ammonia house fed by the ammonia water from the retorts; a gas producer plant with two Dowson and Mason producers that could 'gasify' 24 tons of coal per day; a naphtha plant – this was the only crude works in the area that could refine naphtha; a power station; and steam boilers for all of the above.

Competition was strong, however, both from domestic and imported oil. Many of the original companies failed, in part because of the new, cheap imports – processing crude oil from a well being a markedly less expensive enterprise than shale mining – but often because they were established by people with no experience and little know-how.

One such failure was the Linlithgow Oil Company. Established in 1884, it built a mine, crude oil works and a refinery at Champfleurie, Ochiltree and Kingscavil and was a far bigger operation than Ross. The Government's report for 1896 registered 132 underground and 19 surface workers at Champfleurie while Ochiltree had 168 men underground and 23 on the surface. The mine at Ochiltree was for coal and was situated between the top of the new houses built by the Council in Bridgend in the 1930s and the Ochiltree Road.

(All oil works had sirens to mark the start and end of shifts – there was no point putting them into a mine as they would not be heard in the farthest reaches of the works. The Champfleurie oil works were notorious in the area for the power of their horn – apparently far louder than the rival at Philpstoun; however if reports from the time are to be believed, the Philpstoun pug was just as, if not more, powerful than the Champfleurie engine. Perhaps neither could pull quite as many hutches as the men would have had you believe but suffice it to say that rivalry between the LOC and the Ross men was lively.)

However, so keen had been the Linlithgow Oil Company to start operations that they built their operation 'backwards', the works being established before the railway was put through to join them to Linlithgow station. The connecting railway was eventually put in, the line still clearly visible some 50 years later where it passed under the road between Park Farm and the Troughstone and the sides of its bridge about 100 yards to the west of Bridgend Farm on the Main Road. However the works were almost completed before it was ready and the company could never recoup the massive costs of ferrying all of the building materials to the site by horse and cart.

According to *The Courier* on 7 February 1885, 'it was expected an arrangement would be made with the Linlithgow Oil Co., whereby one railway might suit the requirements of both works' – i.e. an arrangement with Ross for their station also to service the Linlithgow Company. However, 'negotiations with reference to this from some cause or other fell through'.

Added to the fact that Champfleurie proved to produce low-grade shale, and that the management chose not to adapt to new technologies, the Linlithgow Oil Company eventually closed in 1903 and was dissolved in 1904. In 1907, Ross took a lease for 'shale, coal, fireclay and blaes so far as not already worked in the lands of Champfleurie' from the trustees of Captain Stewart. (Blaes was the official name for the burnt shale that formed the massive 'bings' or tips throughout the area. It was also sometimes used to refer to 'fakes' or the layers of unproductive material found in shale seams). Ross also took over the 112 workman's cottages at Kingscavil Rows, Kingscavil store with the house above and, later, the Bridgend houses.

Thus began the era of the infamous three villages, although it must be admitted that the people of Philpstoun always felt that their village was better appointed than the others. People may have moved between the three, but Philpstoun was just better – a sentiment that thrived for decades.

By the time of the Great War, the industry had consolidated into the hands of a few efficient companies. In 1910 they reached a production high of 3.13 million tons of shale output, producing 70 million gallons of crude shale-oil. The war soon checked this growth. Working in oil production did not become a protected job until 1916, by which time many of the men had already left for the front. (Some of the jobs at the time were taken by women, but apparently only surface work). Export markets dried up and it was only through ensuring a secure fuel supply to the Royal Navy and producing ammonia, both sulphate of ammonia for fertiliser for home food production and ammonia for munitions, that the companies survived.

Six oil companies went into the Great War, five came out. Young's (established in 1866), Oakbank (1869), Broxburn (1877), Pumpherston (1883) and Ross

Ross Petrol Post Card
(photograph courtesy of BP)

(1883) survived, the Dalmeny Oil Company (1871) having been taken over by Oakbank in 1916 (it was eventually wound up in 1931). However, by 1919 the companies were less than optimistic about the future. Rising labour and equipment costs, demands for shorter working hours and continued growth in cheaper imports led them to realise that they might not stay afloat on their own for much longer so they approached the Government asking for assistance.

Since 1918 the companies had already been operating common selling arrangements for their products under the umbrella of the Scottish Oils Agency Ltd. In July 1919 this was extended to their manufacturing businesses. The Government had a controlling interest in the Anglo-Persian Oil Company and it now proposed that the latter should have a new subsidiary, Scottish Oils. Although it would not actually take over the five companies, in essence they would be under the joint control of Scottish Oils.

The companies accepted the offer – Ross, by far the smallest, being valued at only £168,750, less than one-eighth of the value of the Pumpherston Company. Anglo-Persian nominated the board of Scottish Oils and the same five men were directors of all five companies, including Robert Crichton of James Ross & Co. as the General Mining Manager.

James Ross & Company Philpstoun Oil Works Limited continued successfully for many years, eventually going into liquidation in February 1936. Its property assets were transferred to the Calderlin Property Company as from the end of 1935 until the latter's own liquidation in 1954 when they were transferred to the Oakbank Oil Company; Oakbank already owned the Whitequarries mines to go along with its works at Duddingston and Westwood by the time that the Government list was drawn up in 1945. Anglo-Persian became the Anglo-Iranian Oil Company in 1935 and then, in 1954, the British Petroleum Company. The Linlithgowshire shale industry would stay active until 1962.

So much for the companies: what about the people?

CHAPTER TWO

The Village Grows

WHEN JAMES ROSS & CO. decided upon Philpstoun to build their works, they were no doubt influenced by the excellent transport links. The railway had arrived in Linlithgow in 1842, when the main Edinburgh and Glasgow Railway was completed, so opening a station at Philpstoun was not too costly a proposition. On 9 September 1884 Ross, the Earl of Hopetoun and the North British Railway Company signed a memorandum of agreement 'as to the proposed passenger station sidings, signal cabin and signals' and Philpstoun station opened in 1885.

(It was to stay open until the 1950s, and was beautifully maintained, even down to its name being picked out in flowers. Over the years, the station was to welcome many an important visitor, perhaps none more imposing than the then richest man in the world, the Shah of Persia on his visit to Hopetoun on 22 July 1889. He was in the area to see the Forth Bridge and arrived on a special train (organised by the venerable Thomas Cook & Sons) in the late afternoon to be greeted on the festooned, red-carpeted platform by the Linlithgowshire Volunteers and their band and, of course, a shower of rain. The Shah was escorted to Hopetoun by mounted police, with the Home Guard and the local constabulary lining the entire route.

According to *The Scotsman*, 'the country people turned out in large numbers, curious no doubt to get a glimpse of the Persian monarch. They lined the roads and hung about the walls and the palings in the vicinity of the station, their numbers being swelled by the arrival of other sightseers from Winchburgh and Linlithgow. They were a quiet and sober crowd and behaved with becoming decorum'. (Quite right too.)

Just as important was the Edinburgh & Glasgow Union Canal, which had been open to navigation since 1822. The canal may have lost most of its passengers to the railway (indeed it was taken over by the North British Railway Company in 1861), but it supported a healthy cargo trade. Sturdy Clydesdale horses would frequently walk the towpaths pulling well-laden barges of sandstone for the building of Edinburgh's New Town and coal from the numerous pits in the region up to Edinburgh, loads soon to be augmented by shale products. (The traffic in the opposite direction was just as useful, if not quite so pleasant:

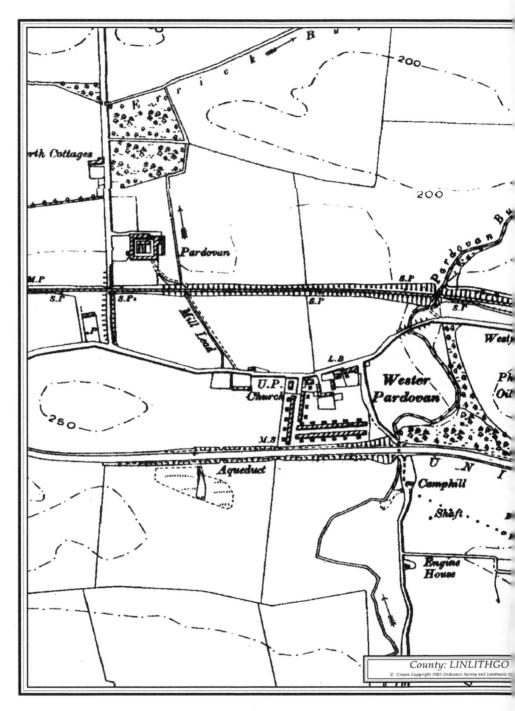

1897 Map

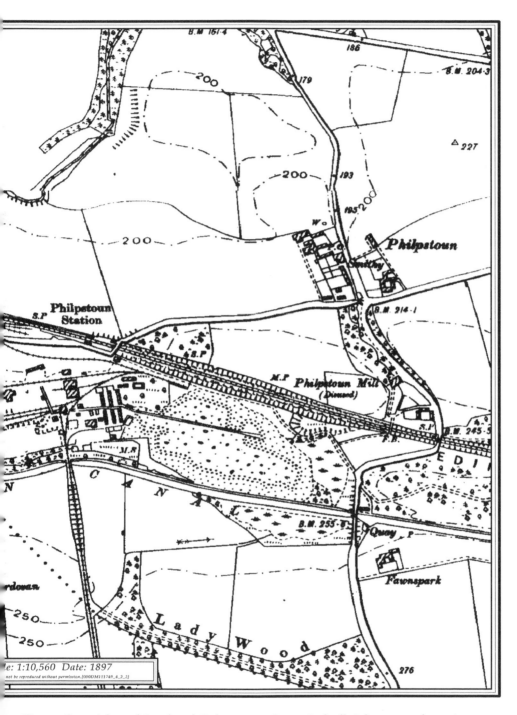

Scale: 1:10,560 Date: 1897

one of the major cargoes of the time was 'police manure', the contents of Edinburgh's dry lavatories that was sent out to the farmers as manure).

A mine is no mine without miners. The local population could not provide a sufficient workforce so imported labour was vital, but thankfully plentiful due to the constant influx of men from the Highlands and the steady stream of job-seeking Irishmen, the latter usually coming on from jobs at the farms and eventually making up about a quarter of the village.

The first under-manager, Mr Gilchrist, brought in a number of seasoned lead miners from his hometown in Wanlockhead, Dumfrieshire, a group of men that soon earned the reputation of being well-educated, religious and generally very respectable. Later the demand for workers was so acute that the company cashier, George (Geordie) Davie, even travelled to Arranmore Island in County Donegal specifically to hire more men, bringing them back to Philpstoun through Glasgow.

To accommodate the workers, Ross took a succession of leases and feu dispositions from the Earl of Hopetoun and in 1885 began to build houses, starting with two rows of two-room cottages on Hope Street (now the site of Church Court). As the mine and oil works were between the station and the canal, it was the name of Philpstoun that attached to the company; however the new village was known as Wester Pardovan, having been built on that farm's lands. The 1901 official report on the water cites the 'Wester Pardovan Rows', 'Hope Street, Wester Pardovan' is the address given in the 1921-1922 valuation roll, 'Wester Pardovan' is cited in many a lease and all Ordnance Survey maps well into the 1950s still clearly show that all of the land west of the Pardovan Burn was indeed Wester Pardovan.

Whatever the official names may have been, apart from some of the older residents who would sometimes refer to Wester Pardovan, the locals had followed their own course and had been referring to the whole as 'Philpstoun' since the early decades of the 20th century, with the original hamlet now demoted to 'Old Philpstoun'. Before the turn of the century Easter Pardovan Farm had become Fairniehill so only Pardovan House and the surrounding area retained the original name and this, together with Pardovan Crescent, the Council housing scheme completed in the 1950s, is now the only remaining use of a name that had survived for centuries.

The Courier carried a description of the 'workman's houses at Philpstoun Oil Works' on 6 June 1885, with the report of the Medical Officer of Health to Linlithgow Town Council about their drainage. He described the houses as 'well constructed; inside walls lined with lathe and plaster; foundations rest on a solid bed', detailed the plan of the drains between them and noted that 'the water for household and washing purposes is being brought to the houses from a burn some distance to the south and east of the houses, the water of which is soft and pure'. Further, the paper reports that 'Dr Gilmour said the houses were the best class of workmen's houses he had ever inspected'. Praise indeed.

There were eventually to be 84 houses in Hope Street, known to all as The Rows: one parallel to the canal and the other leading north, the 'Cross Rows'.

Houses in The Rows were basic, two-room structures, built in blocks of four or six separated by closes. The front, and only, door led into the kitchen (and main living room), which had a coal fireplace, grate and hobs (the only source of heating) and two bed recesses in the wall with storage space, or 'ponds', below, the whole shielded by curtains made by the women. Next to the fireplace was the kitchen press and there were usually a table and chairs, including perhaps one big armchair for Dad, and maybe a sideboard.

The bedroom, known as 'the room', would usually have at least one free-standing bed, perhaps other 'bedroom' furniture and of course a press and a fire-place. It was the most private part of the house, the only way out being through the kitchen, thus it was the perfect place for a quiet evening cup of tea (or homework or any other illicit chore not deemed fit for performance on the Sabbath).

The houses were let unfurnished, but they were equipped with metal bed frames built into the recesses. (In much later years, these were removed and stand-alone beds put in their place. Later still, some residents knocked down the partition between the recesses to make more room).

Mattresses, while expensive, were of course essential. The original residents either bought ready-made straw mattresses – two side-by-side fitting a double bed – or, more cannily, purchased old hundred-weight cotton flour sacks from the miller at Old Philpstoun, bleached them to remove his name and then stuffed them with straw or the chaff left over from the local harvest. A warm and soft bed for each season, remembered affectionately by Miss Hannah Cosgrove as 'nice and comfy'.

Cooking was on the coal-fired range and the oven at its side in the kitchen, in heavy black pots, pans or griddles. The grate always bore a kettle, which was moved into the fire itself when very hot water was needed, and firebricks on the hobs. The grate was almost always warm, so toddlers would be protected by metal fire-screens around the fender, bought by the tenants and polished by the women to within an inch of their brass lives.

There was no water in the original Rows houses, although cold water was piped to the outside washhouses, shared between four or six houses. Kindling fires beneath large iron boilers provided water for cleaning, while a well on the street with a winch bucket, later to be replaced by a standpipe, served as the source of fresh drinking water. The water for the village was supplied by Ross's own water-works, drawn from the burn.

Katie Philbin at the back of
The Rows
(photograph courtesy of K. Philbin)

Behind the houses were ash-pits, individual walk-in coal-houses and shared drying-greens, furnished only with poles so the women would use their own ropes and 'stretchers' to keep them up, which they carefully locked away at night (as would their daughters – stretchers could still be seen in the village up to the 1960s).

Inside toilets were of course unheard of, as was the concept of the flush. There was one outside toilet between two houses, next to the coal-houses, and they were 'dry'. Every week around would come company employees who, to the amusement of the children, would first empty the toilets into their horse's cart and then quite contentedly sit down next to said cart munching their pieces. There were no streetlights in the early village so a night-time trip to the toilet for children was a dark, and terrifying, adventure.

Improvements were made to The Rows houses in 1896 and 1910 and sculleries were attached to the kitchens in 1922. In May 1922, Ross struck an agreement with the Linlithgow Central Water Committee to lay a three inch water pipe in Hope Street to ensure the water supply to The Rows. Henceforth, the house was entered via its one door in the scullery, from where there was a door through to the kitchen (and then another one through to the room). The scullery had a window of frosted glass but it was built so as to partially block the kitchen window, thus making the house slightly darker.

The sculleries had running water, from a tap into a sink – the one sink in the house – and a separate lavatory. They also had a fixed bath and a stone boiler, under which a fire could be kindled to heat water that could be let directly into the bath by a wee tap on its side, although it was rarely used. The cost of boiling so much water was prohibitive and not for such vanities as a bath, so strip washes using water from a boiled kettle continued to be the norm (except for Dad's weekly clean up when the children were shooed from the house to play). Laundry was still done in the wash-houses, where there was more room. The bath had its uses of course, for smaller items of laundry and later its cover served as the stand for an oil stove.

There was a big, walk-in cupboard in the scullery, usually used not to store food but coal pails, brushes, cleaning products and so forth. This pantry also became the permanent home for the man's work clothes, as no self-respecting Philpstoun wife would let such dirty articles into the house proper!

Originally, lighting was by paraffin lamp, effective but not easy given the amount of time needed to keep the glass funnels (or 'globes') clean. Later there was electricity: Philpstoun, like many mining villages, drew its electricity directly from the oil works (on a DC current) and thus had the service well before towns like Edinburgh or Glasgow. Even the oldest Rows houses were wired up in 1922, the residents paying 7d a week for the service.

However, the availability was limited and there was no question of electricity being used for such fripperies as heating or cooking – it was there for light. As one of the notices preserved at the Almond Valley Heritage Centre recalls, even the amount of light was regulated, residents being permitted one 60-watt bulb in the kitchen, one 40-watt bulb in the room, a 30-watt bulb in the scullery and a whopping 15-watt bulb in the lavatory.

There was one small socket in the kitchen, to support a light appliance – trying to connect anything else would have over-powered the 5-amp fuse. Another typical notice preserved at the Centre instructs the tenants that it is for a small appliance, but cautions that:

> only the best quality lamps of British manufacture should be used and tenants are advised not to use cheap lamps of foreign manufacture as these lamps generally use more current.

Later residents could pay for more sockets, but they were solemnly informed that this work should only be undertaken by the trusted workmen of Scottish Oils, not by any other purported electrician.

The Rows were followed by Rosoline Place, Wester Pardovan UF Church (rumoured to have been originally intended as a school) and the Manse. There was also Store Buildings, so called as homes were part of the complex housing the store, on the present-day corner of Gateside and Main Street. The accommodation here was on two levels, rather like a modern-day block of flats. These homes also had two rooms, the usual room and kitchen, with outside washhouses and later sculleries with running cold water and toilets. When the store itself moved to its present site in the 1920s, the whole complex was converted into dwellings.

As soon as a house was ready, it was occupied – there was simply too much call for accommodation to wait for the whole scheme to be completed.

The company also built Castlepark for the family of Mr Archibald Crichton, the Senior Partner of Ross. It was erected in 1896, as were the houses on

Pardovan Church c. 1965
(includes Mr Winton's father and Mr 'Toods' Kilpatrick, photograph courtesy of A Winton via A Jenkinson)

Kinnaird Terrace off the Dairy (the name a throwback to Wester Pardovan Farm and incorporating some of the old farm buildings including two cottages and what was to become the first village hall). The feu disposition for the building of The Neuk on Station Road was taken from the Marquess of Linlithgow in 1909 to provide accommodation for Mr Crichton's son, Robert, upon his marriage the following year.

Further accommodation for the workers became available after the Linlithgow Oil Company went into liquidation. Ross leased the villages of Kingscavil and Bridgend and many of the Linlithgow Company's workers found new positions with the Philpstoun Oil Company. Some workers also lived in the Station Cottages and in 1924 Ross bought the remaining Wester Pardovan Farm land from Hopetoun, including the two cottages at the Dairy.

The Avenue was built in 1910, providing twelve houses for the management and the policemen (in Number 4); essentially the 'smart' part of the village. George Anderson, the Castlepark chauffeur, also lived there. (In later days, the policy would change to allow any workers with larger families to move to The Avenue.)

These houses were of course bigger than those in The Rows, with both front

The Avenue
(photograph courtesy of E Burns)

and back doors, a sitting room, a bedroom, a lobby and a kitchen with a fire, a range and – unknown in The Rows – a boiler with a wee tap to heat water for the dishes. They also had a scullery with a boiler, backing on to a bathroom, a coal cellar, a pantry and a small garden as well as the shared drying-greens. (Hot water was eventually added in the 1950s – a luxury that never made it to The Rows).

Virtually everything in the early days of the village depended on the works. Just to be given a house in Philpstoun, or the other company villages, you had to work for the company. Thereafter, houses were allocated according to the size of the worker's, often extended, family.

Many of the first workers were not from the area, so those among the tenants who had room would take in lodgers. One such example was Mrs McKnight, the beds of whose Rows house around the turn of the 20th Century were said never to be cold, the night shift leaving as the day shift came home. Many another extended family would all squeeze in together, housing being scarce and (relatively) expensive. Despite their limited size, over the years The Rows houses supported surprisingly numerous families, like the Robertsons and their family of twelve – plus two sisters from Glasgow at holidays...

Normal procedure for being allocated a house would be a request to Mr Crichton who, although constantly fair, was certainly no pushover.

Mrs Elizabeth Sweeney well remembers approaching Mr Robert Crichton one evening about the vacancy at number 16 Hope Street after Mrs Russell died. She and her husband Johnny had been renting Granny Davis' room for the last six months and they were hoping for a place of their own. Mr Crichton wasn't convinced and told her that he had been forced to wait until he was 27 before he could marry, so she really should wait a bit longer. Mrs Sweeney pointed out that she was married already, and that her husband was also 27, but at 24 Crichton described her as 'but a wee bit lassie' and she should wait a while before applying for a house. She persevered, and the house was theirs.

That the three villages of Philpstoun, Bridgend and Kingscavil were regarded with pride is perhaps best evidenced by a letter that RG Philip, Minister of Pardovan Church, sent to the editor of the socialist magazine *John Bull* on 20 December 1935. On 16 November the magazine, which prided itself on exposing the scandals of the day, had carried an article describing 'distressed areas', including the shale field in this part of Linlithgow parish. Mr Philip was not impressed.

While correcting the author's geography, explaining that the villages were in West, not Mid, Lothian and that they were not 'tucked away in the mountains miles from anywhere' but very close to both main road and railway, Mr Philip did accept that 'there has been a very regrettable decline in the shale industry'. He also agreed that there was 'a crying need for replacing the houses and sanitary arrangements in Bridgend and Kingscavil'.

However, he totally refuted the notion that the area could be home to 'anything like 12,000 families' when there were only 1,023 voters on the roll. Indeed at the time that the shale industry was at its height, there were some 10,000 workers – not families – employed in the whole shale field. The Reverend went on to note that the district was 'remarkably healthy'. In 1934, the death rate for this part of Linlithgow parish was '9.3 per 1,000 of the population' and 'four years ago there were only 4 TB cases (notified) in the district: at present there are only 2'. That Bridgend had been 'specially singled out for mention' was also unmerited given that 'the district nurse is able to report that it is the healthiest village of the three'.

Mr Philip was equally unimpressed with the magazine's description of the houses, firmly stating that it 'does not apply to Philpstoun at all. It is a very clean and relatively up-to-date village' – the journalist apparently having chosen to overlook the fact that sculleries, 'modern conveniences' and electric lighting had been added to the original houses 'a number of years ago'.

It was true that the Kingscavil and Bridgend houses were older, having been built some 50 years previously, but repairs to them had been 'constantly carried out'. More importantly, 'the houses have now been condemned under the Clearance scheme, and steps are being taken by the County Council to replace them by one village of 180 houses or more on an airy site on the hillside close to Bridgend'. (A scheme of 184 houses was in fact completed in 1937, replacing the 92 miners' homes condemned by the Department of Health.) Not only

Peter and Grace Mushet
(photograph courtesy of P Mushet)

that, this was for the benefit of the people, not the company, as 'this site has the definite drawback of not being close to any work, and bus fares will have to be paid, or cycles used, by those who will be in employment, but it was the choice of the people themselves'.

The Reverend went on to clarify that 'there is no licensed house in Bridgend or Philpstoun although there is one in Kingscavil. Each village has its football ground, and at Philpstoun there is a well-built recreative Institute, a bowling green, and two tennis courts'. There were also allotments at Bridgend and eight acres of the same at Philpstoun 'in the hands of about twenty holders or more'.

Of course, unemployment was still a problem and 'it is not possible to forecast the future [of the Scottish shale industry] with certainty'. However 'an increase of five per cent in the wages of those employed has just been announced. It may be added that a large number of girls from the district obtain good situations in domestic service in Edinburgh and elsewhere'.

Poor they may have been, but no-one was going to call them 'distressed'.

Although the new houses at Bridgend were owned by the Council and not Scottish Oils, given his contacts on the Council Robert Crichton was not above helping out there too if there was good reason. Peter Mushet, for example, may not have qualified for a house just for him and wife Grace, but when he explained to Mr Crichton about Grace's three brothers and one sister who were coming along too, Mr Crichton helped them to secure a Bridgend house. (Not that Grace was happy about that. She desperately wanted to come back to Philpstoun, so much so that when she pushed her pram under the bridge she 'couldn't see for tears'... some time later, the family moved back to the village. Once a Philpstouner...)

Business has always thrived on detail. Ross signed multiple agreements over the years for small pieces of land, new buildings, new feu duties – everything in the village had to be granted over somehow. Everything. Take this as an example: in 1918 and 1919 Ross and the North British Railway Company struck an agreement regarding the 'fence on the south side of Wester Pardovan village... The Hedge and Trees to be removed by James Ross & Co. Philpstoun Oil Works Ltd., a Wooden Fence similar to one at the Goods Station, Philpstoun, to be erected and maintained by James Ross & Co. in lieu of the Hedge and to be replaced by an unclimbable Iron Fence at the request of the Railway Company any time after the Wooden Fence has been erected for three years. A gate to be erected near each end of Fence. Fence to extend down to Pardovan Burn'.

It is heartening, is it not, to see how seriously Ross took its responsibilities.

CHAPTER THREE

The Cast

IT WOULD, OF COURSE, be impossible to list all of Philpstoun's residents during the days of the mines, but some characters simply cannot be forgotten, nor the village's story told without them.

The most important family in the village by far was the Crichtons. The Glasgow-born Archibald H Crichton JP became a partner in James Ross & Co. in the mid-1880s after training as a mining engineer and working in a number of other positions in the industry, including with the famed Young's Paraffin Light and Mineral Oil Company. A self-made, sombre and industrious man, he was also, according to the Philpstoun women who worked at Castlepark, a very strict father.

In correspondence relating to the dispute over the miners' wages reproduced in *The West Lothian Courier* on 26 March 1887, John Wilson, Secretary of the Shale Miners' Union, described Mr Crichton thus:

> *As a man Mr Crichton is superior regarding his mental and particularly his conversational powers. He is an ardent temperance reformer, and, if I mistake not, a pillar in the church, but it is well known to a considerable number of people outside of the mines that he is largely touched with pride and ambition and that his manner generally is haughty and imperious. Like many other men in his position he is virtually the ruler of Philpstoun [sic] hamlet.*

Few anecdotal tales of this Mr Crichton survive, except his disagreement with the content of a sermon at Pardovan Church. Rising up, he informed the Minister of his error then turned and marched his family out of the church. For the rest of the Crichtons' time in Philpstoun, they would worship at St Michael's in Linlithgow, a snub felt not least in the collection box of Pardovan which had lost its only rich parishioner.

Robert Crichton was far from being the spoilt son of the boss. When he gave up his original idea to become a doctor and exhibited interest in following in his father's footsteps, Archibald may not have stood in his way, but neither did he pull the proverbial strings. Robert wanted to be in the shale business? Then he could learn how it worked. His father gave him a job as a pit pony lad.

Robert was not to be deterred so took himself off to night school to train as a mining engineer, finishing his studies at Heriot-Watt, probably never dreaming that in later life he was to serve as a Governor to this very College for ten years and even to be awarded an honorary Fellowship in 1952.

Robert was to become Mining Manager and Assistant to the Managing Director of Ross by at least 1908, ten years before the death of his father. He served in the Territorials during the Great War and when Ross was subsumed into Scottish Oils Robert went too, as General Mining Manager. He became a Director of Scottish Oils in 1928 and Managing Director in 1941, only to retire in 1954. Most of this work thus covers the period of tenure of Mr Robert Crichton JP, CBE.

With his wife, who came from Linlithgow Bridge and had been a teacher at Bridgend (needless to say, Archibald did not approve of the match!), Robert had two sons (Archie and Bobby) and two daughters (Anne and Margaret). Shale, of course, played a part in their upbringing: the Crichton family still have a piece of shale dug up by Archie on his first visit down a mine in January 1918 and another piece was presented to Bobby when he and his new bride were taken down the mine after their wedding in 1949. (None of the children pursued a career in the oil industry, Archie going on to become a doctor and Bob, after five years in the army and being awarded an MC for his bravery in the Italian campaign, going on to the Edinburgh and East of Scotland College of Agriculture where he was to meet his wife, a lecturer in agricultural botany, before becoming a tenant farmer).

From his home at Castlepark, Mr Robert Crichton was very much in charge of all he surveyed, including the works, houses and comportment of the people in all of the company villages. He took his moral position very seriously – even down to prohibiting the hanging out of washing on Sundays.

Despite being in a position of ultimate authority, it seems that Mr Crichton was a 'benevolent despot' who was universally respected, in some ways the 'father of the village'. In the 50 years that Jean and Agnes Allan came in from their home at Store Buildings to work in Castlepark, they never had ill to report – indeed, given his incredibly strict upbringing their colleague Mrs Stein was even known to comment that it was a wonder he had turned out so well.

The village children were happy to roll their Easter eggs in his back garden (and to steal his apples but that, perhaps, rather less obviously). As well as coming up to Castlepark to ask for houses, the villagers would also frequently come for job references, to ask Mr Crichton to present prizes to the sports clubs, for charity collections or even to sing carols. His name may have inspired awe, even fear, in the men, but he was certainly not a cruel man. Stories live on of how he made it clear that anyone found making fun of a mentally slow boy

Group Photo

Back row: James Burns, Peter Swan, Willie Allen, ??, George Anderson (Mr Crichton's chauffeur), ??, ??, John Ford
Middle row: Jock Muir, Jean Allen, ??, Agnes Allen, ?Ramsay, ?Readdie
Front row: Neil Campbell, Miss Crichton, Mrs Crichton, Bob Crichton, Mr Crichton, Mary Stirton, Elum Anderson, George Muir *(photograph courtesy of E Burns)*

employed at the mine would be fired and how he gave a full suit of clothes to a tramp at his door.

He also looked after his villagers: if any man from the villages died, his widow would be sure to receive a wreath from the Crichtons. He visited the family of the Gala Day Queen – Mrs Katie Philbin remembers the look of delight on the face of her daughter Kathleen (little sister to the 1949 incumbent, Margaret) when he gave her the princely sum of 10 shillings. He even went so far as to arrange that an early bus be put on after the Second World War so that the village girls, heading to jobs in offices and shops, no longer had to walk up to Gateside to catch the Edinburgh connection.

The respect in which he was held was well evidenced by the imposing silver salver presented to Mr and Mrs Crichton on their silver wedding anniversary in April 1935 by 'past and present employees of James Ross & Co.' and the equally impressive canteen of silver cutlery from the officials of Scottish Oils. According to the BP magazine of June 1954, upon Mr Crichton's retirement a local paper noted, 'he didn't believe in personnel managers: it was his own job to see his men were happy and that's the sort of thing that we miners don't forget'. Modern management gurus take note.

Mr and Mrs Robert Crichton's Silver Wedding, 1935
Miss Wilson, D Munro, James Burns, Mr & Mrs Crichton.
(*photograph courtesy of Bob Crichton*)

The 'glen' behind Castlepark (known as Crichton's Wood to the villagers) provided the perfect setting for a family tennis court (until it was washed away by the burn in full flood) and dens for the boys. It was also, unbeknown to the miners, where some of the workings were just below the surface. Bob Crichton remembers the day that his father and he were walking on the surface and could clearly hear the voices of the men working underground; quite what they thought when they heard the voice of Robert Crichton joining in their conversation and addressing them apparently from the very face itself remains unrecorded.

Mr Crichton was very much involved in village life – he frequently played bowls, gave speeches and attended functions in the hall – but the villagers most often saw him surveying his territory from the back of his car as Willy McWhiston or George Anderson chauffeured their boss from meeting to mine. He was frequently down one or other of the mines for an inspection (as can be verified by Ian Smith, in latter years architect and civil engineer with BP but as an apprentice at Middleton Hall, Scottish Oils' administrative HQ at Uphall, many years ago it was his responsibility to prepare Mr Crichton's hot bath, soap and towels after such visits. For this service, he was presented with Mr Crichton's cap lamp).

During the course of nearly 60 years in the oil business, Robert Crichton was to prove himself a man to be reckoned with. As well as his position with Scottish Oils he was: a Director of Grangemouth Refinery and of British Hydro-Carbon Chemicals Ltd; a Fellow of the British Institute of Petroleum and the first Chairman of its Scottish branch; Chairman of the Institute of Mining Electrical and Mechanical Engineers; Governor of the Royal Technical College, Glasgow; a Member of West Lothian County Council, including 10 years as the County Convenor; the first Chairman of Bangour Hospital's Board of Management; a Member of the Board of St Michael's Hospital; and a Senior Elder of St Michael's Church. In 1952 he was, hardly surprisingly, awarded the CBE for services to industry and the country.

Mr Crichton eventually retired in March 1954. On 23 March, a tribute evening was held at Middleton Hall with about 200 attendees. This was followed on 2 April 1954 with a 'Testimonial to Robert Crichton Esquire, JP, from members of the public in Philpstoun and District' held in the Philpstoun village hall.

When Robert Crichton moved his family to Castlepark, The Neuk became home to Robert (Bert) Keddie, Scottish Oils' agent (or area manager for the mines) and Crichton's protégé. He and his wife hailed from Winchburgh and made a very handsome couple – Mrs Keddie was famed for a wardrobe that reputedly ran the entire length of the wall.

The local under-manager was James Burns, the son of the blacksmith at Burnside. He had left school in 1902 at the age of 14 and like many of his pals gone straight to the mines, but later took his manager's certificate at Heriot-Watt. He and his wife waited to marry until after the Great War, after which they moved to Blackness and then to Number 1, The Avenue. A keen sportsman, Mr Burns gave several talks in later years to the Philpstoun Boys' Club at the request of the Minister Mr Nicholson, recording some early memories of village life on paper (for which certain amateur historians are very grateful).

George (Geordie) Davie, the company cashier, came to Ross from the Linlithgow Oil Company. He too was a keen sportsman, representing Philpstoun on the Linlithgow Bowling Association, becoming Vice President of the West Lothian Cricket Club and, according to his obituary in *The Courier* on 25 August 1933, he 'was responsible for many musical programmes in connection with the Recreation Club. He also rendered notable service to Philpstoun and District Nursing Association of which he was secretary and treasurer'.

The police station, and home to the constables Moir, Rintoul, Weir, Forbes, Wood then Ramsay, was at Number 4, The Avenue. Prior to 1919, the West Lothian County Council paid an annual rent for this house to Ross of £16, which went up to £22/8/3d as from 1920 (less occupiers' local rates which the Council kindly waived on houses occupied by police constables) when electric lighting was added to the houses.

While it is hard to believe that policing the village was an overly difficult duty, Saturday night, and the infamous return of many of the men from the Linlithgow pubs, did provide the odd set-to. Not that it was worth trying to get Johnny Moir to come out after 10pm to calm down the Irishmen – you would simply be told that the priest would do a better job so some poor soul would be given the task of cycling up to Linlithgow to fetch him.

(There was a telephone at the police station through which important messages, like births and deaths, would arrive. Other telephones in the village by the time of the Second World War, according to the ARP list, were at the store, the station, Pardovan Number 7 and, obviously, Castlepark and The Neuk. The telephone kiosk did not appear until 1946, the agreement for its erection being signed between Scottish Oils and Post Office Telephones Edinburgh on 22 June.)

It wasn't just the management who are remembered. There was Jimmy the Scaffy, Jimmy Paterson, who was employed by Scottish Oils to keep the village tidy, sweeping the streets, picking up litter, emptying the bins into his horse's cart, cutting the grass and so forth. Although he never touched them, and did nothing worse than scowl, he terrified the children by his mean manner. (Later the job was taken by Johnny Ward.)

Souvenir Programme

Testimonial to

Robert Crichton Ogston, J.P.

FROM MEMBERS OF THE PUBLIC
IN PHILPSTOUN AND DISTRICT

AT THE HALL, PHILPSTOUN
ON FRIDAY, 2nd APRIL, 1954

CHAIRMAN · · · MR R. KEDDIE

COMMITTEE MEMBERS

Mr Robert Keddie, *Hon. President*
Mr Arch. Gilmour, *Hon. Secretary*
Mr William Allan, *Hon. Treasurer*

Mr D. Ramsay	Mr D. Munro
Mr A. Orr	Mr J. Orr
Mr J. Ward	Mr R. McKenna
Mr R. Neilson	Mr B. Grant
Mr J. Muir	Mr A. Manson
Mr W. Currie	Mr W. Watson
Mr J. Wishart	Mr D. Walker
Mr J. Cameron	Mr A. McKenzie
Mr John Burns	Mr G. Hume

HOSTESSES

Mrs Readdie	Mrs Allan
Mrs Gilmour	Mrs Watson
Miss Allan	Miss J. Allan
Miss Dunn	Mrs Kilpatrick
Mrs Moir	Mrs Stein
Mrs Grant	Mrs Muir
Mrs Ford	Mrs Anderson
Miss Neilson	Mrs Stirton

Mr Crichton's Testimonial Programme, 1954
(autographed by him)

Artists

Mrs R. McDonald	Soprano
Mr Philip Powell	Tenor
Mr George Fleming	Bass
Miss Pearl Burrows	Elocutionist
Mr James Armstrong	Violinist
Mr Frank Murrie	Accompanist

VOTES OF THANKS

Artistes - - -	Mr John Burns
Reply - -	Mr Murrie
Committee and Hostesses -	Chairman
Chairman -	Mr John Orr

9.45 p.m. Auld Lang Syne

Programme

7.0 p.m.	Introductory Remarks -	Mr Robert Keddie
	Blessing.	
	Tea.	
7.30 p.m.	INTERVAL	
7.45 p.m.	The Chairman - -	Mr Robert Keddie
	Presentation to Mr R. Crichton	Mr Jas. Burns
	Reply - -	Mr R. Crichton
	Presentation to Mrs R. Crichton	Mrs William Allan
	Reply - -	Mrs R. Crichton
	Tributes from :	
	Miss A. Wilson	
	Mr David Munro	

Other well-known faces included: Will Davidson and his pipes, who would frequently pick up a prize at the highland games or other championships; Johnny Docherty, the miner who turned hairdresser by night; and Doctor Carter from Linlithgow who was infamous for never wearing socks as 'they were just a harbour for fleas'. Then there were the old Irishmen who would never pass a body on the street without wishing them the 'top of the morning'.

Every village has its much-loved characters, and Philpstoun around the wars could boast no better than The Laird, the Irishman Paddy Ward. Universally liked, he was a local legend of the best kind – the sort with the sayings that are passed from generation to generation. The natural wit of the Irish, some would say.

There was the time that a stranger walked into the Star and Garter in Linlithgow, recognised him as they had been at school together and asked the barman to send him up a dram. His reply: 'impossible, there had been no man at the school with him that had a black moustache'. It was the Laird who took a bus from Gateside with Johnny Sweeney to attend a wake at Kingscavil without the address, so chapped a door and asked 'is this where the dead man lives?', and he too that terrified the women during the Second World War by telling them not to bother coming out of the air-raid shelter as the whole place was flattened to the ground.

Perhaps the favourite tale of all, however, is about the scarf he bought in Falkirk, thinking it green, later to discover it blue. His wife told him to return it, so he did – claiming that it was 'too tight'.

Philpstoun men at the bottom of The Rows (1940s/50s)

Standing: James Savage (authors' grandfather/father), Eddie Boyle, Johnnie Ward, ? Kerr, Paddy McArdle, Davey McKenzie

Front: Frank Gartland, ? Sutherland, ? Russell, Will Currie, ??, (?? child), Ben Scott, ??, Dick Grant, ??

(photograph B Pattullo)

CHAPTER FOUR

Life as a Shale Miner

ONCE THE VILLAGE BOYS turned 14 and left school, there was no real question of what they would do: they approached the manager of the works and were virtually guaranteed a job. (There was really nothing else to do – Scottish Oils would not allow any light industry to be established in the area that could have purloined their workforce). They would normally hope to work their way up – perhaps starting with lighter work at the brick works or oncosts, or as a pit pony lad, moving to the pithead, then down to the couplings before they started drawing off from a faceman. Perhaps one day they would even get a face of their own to work.

Intelligence, aptitude and choice had no role to play and the boys ended up wherever there was an opening. Neither was there formal training; they learnt on the job. There were, of course, trades in the mine – electricians, joiners, blacksmiths – but no boy from The Rows could ever aspire to such a position. You had to be someone to be a tradesman.

Philpstoun Oil Works
(photograph courtesy of BP)

The original Philpstoun mine, oil works, retorts and bing (the tip of spent shale) were between the station and the canal, on land leased from Hopetoun. Known as 'Number 1', the mine was Ross's first and the workplace of most of the village men in the early days, later to be followed by workings at Whitequarries, Bridgend, Duddingston, Totleywells and so on. (Philpstoun and Whitequarries linked up underground, they were so close.)

The brick works were built in 1920 and produced sand-lime bricks using the spent shale from the bing. This was one of the first uses for the tips which were until then regarded as economically useless and really rather unsightly. This new enterprise was given the name of the British Brick Company Ltd and took a lease from Ross for 25 years as from 1 December 1920. However, it went into liquidation on 27 December 1927.

Water for the Philpstoun works came from the Union Canal under an agreement between the North British Railway Company and Ross. A further agreement allowed Ross to use canal water as a stand-by should the oil engine that ran the village lighting break down, an arrangement that continued until Martinmas 1938 when the Power Company took over the role of supplying the village's electric current.

Unlike coal, shale is not usually so far underground as to require pit mines. There were some pits in the area however, such as those at Threemiletown – Number 35, behind the Red Rows (which proved to be a mistake as it was sunk too low for the shale, so the men had to work upwards to find the seams) – and Whitequarries – Number 6. Except in these mines, where the men were taken underground in cages, the workers originally just walked down from the surface; in later more safety-conscious days they were taken down by railway carriages.

Being so close to the surface, subsidence was always a worry with shale mines so they were generally dug well away from buildings. (Some of the mines had escape hatches, but these were not often used except when some of the men fancied a wee bit of clandestine fresh air.) An example of the havoc that mines could wreak on the landscape is still evident at Hopetoun: no. 41 mine at Fawnspark collapsed, leaving one area far higher than the surrounding field. Even being in the country they could create problems – more than one field collapsed into tunnels. Still, at least all of Hope Street had turnips for tea those nights.

The genesis of the mine would be the blasting out the 'dook', the first opening, and the establishment of the main haulage – a sort of main road from which the levels (like side streets) led to the individual workings at regular intervals. The levels would then be joined together by 'upsets' in a grid pattern.

The main haulage would be fitted out with a railway – laid by the roadmen – and end in a 'T-junction'. It would be equipped with an endless rope to pull the full 'hutches' (or 'bogies', wagons of shale) up to the surface. In the deepest parts of the mine the oncostmen – the haulage team – would hitch the full hutches to the pit ponies to pull them from the workings to the main haulage and then clip them on to the rope; further up, where there were no ponies, this was the job of the men.

Shale is far too hard to mine with picks so has to be blasted out, and it was the responsibility of the faceman so to do. Setting his shoulder to his ratchet borer (electric drills did not come along until the 1930s) the faceman would drive shot holes about 6 feet into the wall. First would come the 'dipper' – centre bottom – then two further holes on either side, about a foot apart. Next, two holes above at middle height – the 'breasts' – then two above at the top.

After cleaning them out with a copper scraper, the faceman would take his wooden 'stemmer' and pack the holes with a gunpowder cartridge and fuse, using gunpowder that he bought himself from the Co-op in wee blue bags. In the early days there was not much ceremony about this, the gunpowder being delivered, as was everything, by horse and cart and sold by the weight and then kept somewhere or other at home. Later the miners would collect it from the pithead, with the cost docked from their wages.

Given the amount of explosives employed, there were of course numerous accidents. Indeed in 1902 the Inspector of Mines stated that 'the shale mines are responsible for the larger proportion of accidents by explosives relative to output and this need not be wondered at, considering the quantity of explosives used and the number of shots fired in the mining operations'. In just one case example Robert Barnes, aged 50, lit three shots together in the Philpstoun mine in 1902. The resulting explosion broke his leg and caused many other injuries and despite crawling 150 feet up a 1 in 4 incline to safety, he later died. So concerned were the authorities that they established a Special Rule limiting the number of shots to be fired at any one time to two.

After the face was blasted apart – largest charges for the bottom section, smaller ones at the top – the faceman would move in to check that all was safe, shoring up any suspect sections with 'trees' (wooden props) topped with 'clugs' (small cross beams). He and his drawer would then clear the space needed for them to lay the rail into the level and the drawer would get on with his task of 'drawing off' from the faceman: filling the hutches with the blasted rock and pulling them to the ponies to take them on to the main haulage.

They would keep driving in, propping up the roof with trees every 4 feet or so until they had a corridor about 12 feet wide and 6 feet high – all of which without the benefit of any sort of ear protection. The authors would hereby like to register their amazement that the former miners they interviewed could hear any of the questions posed.

All of the faceman's tools – the boring machine, set of drills, shovels and picks, together his 'graith' – were his own and would be left in the mine at the end of his shift; there was no question of theft. Only later did the company start to provide tools, such as electric drills.

Shale lies in diagonal seams so the faceman would follow it in a straight line, uphill, until his workings met up with others in a room (or 'upset') usually around 60 feet by 100 feet around a central unworked pillar (or 'stoop'). He would then retrace his steps, or 'step back', letting the tunnels collapse and collecting the props as he went, taking the broken clugs home as fuel, before starting all over again somewhere else. (If there was ever a time when the mine was likely to collapse, it was during stepping back when the integrity of the workings was weakened.) This 'stoop and room' form of shale mining was the most common and resulted essentially in a grid system underground. At any one time there could be between 200 and 300 men working in a mine.

The facemen contracted to provide a certain amount of shale to the company (hence they were also known as 'contractors') and were paid by the ton. Once the hutches reached the surface their contents would be carefully weighed by the inspector (or 'crowpicker'), with useless rock being discounted. The hutches would be marked so that they could be attributed to the right faceman and the men often jointly employed a 'checkweighman' to ensure the measurements were fair.

The faceman alone received a weekly pay packet from the company and it was up to him to pay his drawer. There was a minimum amount, based on the contracted tonnage; thereafter, he paid his drawer whatever he thought appropriate. Needless to say the pay varied with the faceman and it was not unheard of for the drawer to be paid only 'scab wages' – the bare minimum – or even to be left without his money on those weeks when his faceman had gambled away his earnings. Then again, a decent faceman would pay his drawer a fair share of any extra that they had delivered 'on their own can' – beyond the contracted amount. All of the men's wages would fluctuate depending on the price that the oil was making on the markets.

Once emptied, the hutches were sent back down the haulage, one pit prop in each to keep the facemen supplied. The men would also happily hitch a ride in the empty hutches if they were going their way.

Meanwhile, up on the surface the blasted shale was broken up and crushed into roughly fist-sized pieces to increase the surface area and then heated to about 600 degrees Celsius in huge retorts, a process which turned the kerogen trapped between the layers of shale into vapour. This vapour was collected, cooled and condensed into a liquid – crude oil – which was then refined by virtue of different boiling points into various end products (like petrol), a simple technique called fractional distillation.

Originally, Philpstoun Oil Works had retorting capability. In later years, however, the hutches from the Philpstoun mine were pulled by rail engines ('pugs'), or even certain endless ropes, either to the Niddry Castle Oil Works at Winchburgh to be retorted or directly to Pumpherston – the only refinery in the Lothians by 1934. The shale from Duddingston and Whitequarries was also sent to Winchburgh to be retorted.

(It is still easy to see where these railway lines led away from the site of the old works. In fact, many of the straight 'footpaths' that cut across country today used to be the old 'bogie lines'. For example, walk east out of the village along the canal, and turn right up the path towards Burnside: that was the line to Number 7 mine at Bridgend. At the top of the line, it would pass over the main road, the level crossing being protected by big gates.)

The Pug
(*John Doherty, photograph courtesy of Jim Doherty*)

After the oil was extracted, the spent shale was dropped from the retorts into hutches which were hauled up and tipped over the sides of the ubiquitous pink bings that used to mark the whole area, although notably not at White-quarries as, being close to Hopetoun, the tips there were always cleared away. (Many of these bings have now been carried away to start new lives as foundations for motorways and other construction projects.)

Although no first-hand accounts of life for the earliest Philpstoun Oil Company workers have survived (at least, not to the knowledge of the authors!), Patrick Gallagher did mention several villages in the area in his autobiography. Later to be known as Paddy the Cope for his pioneering work with the Co-operative movement in Donegal, Paddy came to Scotland in the late 1880s and worked carrying bricks for the building of the new retorts at Niddry. He earned threepence halfpenny an hour for working ten hours a day, and paid 2/6d a week for lodgings, including bed, soap and milk for his tea.

Porridge and milk for supper were ninepence a week and other foods would either be bought by the worker or by the landlady on his behalf, and would of course be guarded proprietarily. Paddy told of beef (a relatively cheap meat thus part of the staple diet) being carefully cut into even measures and tied with string, so that when boiled equal shares would be lifted out of the pan.

Later Paddy moved to 'very warm work' in the retorts. Red-hot shale was dropped from the retorts into hutches, which were then pulled by two men from the neck of the retort to the endless chain that would take them to the bings. (Burning accidents were common for the men working at the retorts.) There were three shifts: six to nine, ten to one and two to five o'clock, seven days a week, for which the daily pay was 4/-.

The next year, he moved to the Glendevon shale mine as a drawer, earning 4/6d a shift, work he found much better than the retorts and he stayed there until the Broxburn strike of the early 1890s when he returned to Ireland.

Coming back to Scotland later with his wife, Paddy lodged in Uphall for a time, in a worker's house with the familiar room and kitchen that was home to no less than eight lodgers already. The mistress of the house and Paddy's wife shared the bed in the kitchen while the men slept in the room, several at a time depending on their shifts. (It seems that the Uphall Rows were not so well equipped as those in Philpstoun as they had no 'outhouses', but a common yard between about 20 houses with a central wall to separate men from women).

No miner's life has ever been easy. Well into the first decades of the 20th Century, there were 364 workdays in a year, the only exception being 1 January, but many chose to work for the extra money. Christmas was a workday like any other, although some took the day as a holiday to go to church – an observance for which they were docked a day's pay. Later, Christmas was also an official holiday, but it was still unpaid. Hogmanay was celebrated by the village with first footing and general goodwill but no great party – after all, there was no money for such excess, or time for recovery.

Standard working weeks in the early days would be some 60 hours for the miners and up to 72 for the engine-men. Some considered this excessive, and called upon the management to consider idle days.

On 23 April 1887, *The West Lothian Courier* carried a report of a general meeting of the miners held at Philpstoun Oil Works the preceding Monday afternoon. Two men had approached Mr Archibald Crichton, saying that they had been appointed by a meeting to tell him that they would like an idle day on a coming Thursday, apparently because some of the men wanted to attend a meeting of the Miners' Association in Linlithgow.

Mr Crichton was of course sure that this meeting had been 'a small one and in no way representative of the miners in the work' and that 'they proposed what was opposed to the desire of the majority of the men', so he had called this meeting. Here, he said that:

> *months ago he had explained to many of the men, and to several dep-utations, the circumstances at the works, which rendered general idle days at the mines undesirable, while work at the retorts was going on: and from the renewed regularity of work at the mines, he had come to believe that the facts conveyed to the men had so impressed them on the subject that consorted idle days had become a thing of the past at these works. There seemed, however, still to be a few of the men who did not understand the explanations that had been made from time to time as affording reason why general and untimely idle days should cease...*

The result was not difficult to predict. Mr Crichton submitted that the men 'declare themselves opposed to consorted idle days and in favour of each man taking an idle day as it suited himself and his work', a proposal that was 'unanimously and heartily approved of'. Everyone was at work on Thursday.

By the 1930s, things were a little easier. There were two shifts that the men worked week about – the day shift (7am until 2pm) and the back shift (2-10 pm), unless they worked in the retorts or the oil works where there was also a night shift as constant staffing was essential. Sundays were holidays and Saturdays half days, finishing at 12 noon.

Some shale was always tipped before it was processed to ensure a reserve in case of need. This provided extra work, and pay, for any men willing to work on New Year's Day, who would spend the day 'working at the bing', shovelling shale into the retorts to be paid, as ever, by the tonnage.

Apart from the train and occasional horses and carts, there was one main mode of transport in the beginning, to work or anywhere: feet. Bicycles appeared later and many of the men went to work this way, on contraptions frequently held together by string and shoelaces. Some had no tyres, so there was no need of a bell – they were heard long before they were seen. When the Philpstoun works closed and getting to Winchburgh made a bike all the more important, Coby Watson remembered that those of the lads who could ride gave lessons to the others down the back of The Rows.

For workers coming in from Linlithgow, the train was the most practical option so in February 1917 Ross struck a deal with the North British Railway Company (which would become part of the London and North Eastern Railway in 1923) for a special 'workman's train'. With Ross guaranteeing the railway company £5 a week (it expected about 150 men to travel), the service started on 5 March 1917, leaving Linlithgow at 6.15am with return tickets costing 3d. The next year, Ross again approached the railway company, this time about running a train from Philpstoun to Linlithgow on Saturdays. For a guarantee of 15/- the railway agreed and this new service started on 9 November 1918.

In the 1920s, relations between the rail and oil companies became rather more strained. In 1925, Middleton Hall (Scottish Oils' HQ) was not impressed that the guarantee for both trains was now £15 per week, with tickets at 2d single and 5d return, so they stopped the service until the railway company reduced the guarantee again. The days of the special Saturday train were eventually to come to an end when an ordinary passenger train from Edinburgh to Falkirk started to run on Saturday afternoons, arriving at Philpstoun at 2pm (as from 4 December 1926). Ross, obviously, cancelled the special train and the guarantee was reduced even further.

That guarantee didn't last for long either. When the bus service improved, Ross pointed out to the railway company that its men could now come out from Linlithgow by bus, for the same fare as they paid on the train. On 25 April 1927, down came the guarantee again. Eventually, on 2 March 1929, they gave up on running the special trains altogether – the buses were taking over.

(The bus companies like Massons of Broxburn didn't only take the men to work of course, they were also there for the women or for any trip out – presuming the villagers were happy to walk up to the stop at Gateside. When the SMT started, there was a price war with Massons, so the locals would cannily check with the drivers who was the cheaper today before they boarded).

The mine's day would begin at 5am with a safety check by the firemen (in particular for gas) and assuming all was clear the men would start heading down at 7 o'clock. They were supervised by the under-manager during the day shift and a fireman thereafter, although the under-manager could of course always be called back in case of need.

The miners did not come back up to the surface between the start and end of a shift. Kitted out in steel toe-capped tackety boots with bo-yanks tied around their moleskin trousers (to stop the rats running up their legs), a waistcoat (with a pit watch and a wee tin box of Woodbines cigarettes in the pocket) and a heavy coat, they would set off to the mine carrying their tin piece boxes and tin tea flasks (no point using a thermos, it would only break). Wearing a helmet wasn't compulsory so most preferred the comfort of their cloth caps.

In an action that would send a modern health and safety inspector to the cardiac ward, once underground the miners would put white chips of calcium carbide (bought at the store) into an open tin attached to their cloth caps, adjust the regulator at the top of this 'lamp' so that water dripped on to the chips and then light the resultant gas. A cloth cap topped with a naked flame, often worn by a chap contentedly smoking a cigarette... Carbide lamps certainly gave excellent light, but their demise is unlikely to be sadly lamented.

The only time that the use of carbide lamps was forbidden and the men had to rely on alternative lighting, like the battery-operated 'Nife' electric lamps that came along between the wars, was if the deadly gas Black Damp (or Fire/Choke Damp – carbonic acid or methane) was suspected. (Gas is just as common in shale workings as in coal, but shale does not produce the inflammable dust found in coal mines.) Once the fireman declared the workings safe, the men would have no hesitation using naked flames or smoking underground.

Gas could be detected by the faceman's 'Glenney' lamp, the flame of which turned blue in the presence of noxious air, and there was always the tried and tested method of bringing down the canaries (kept at the top of the mine for just such eventualities) to see if their feathers ruffled. If gas was found, the usual dispersal method was simply to cut off lengths of white screen-cloth and waft them around the suspect area, or bring in an extra fan.

It was gas that caused the industry's worst disaster at Burngrange, Midlothian. In 1947, a miner's cap carbide lamp ignited gas in a roof cavity and 15 men were trapped as a result of the explosion, dying when the oxygen ran out. There were thankfully no disasters of the same magnitude in the Philpstoun district mines, but there were of course some terrible accidents, reported to the surface by the pit telephone; there were no sirens to alert the village.

In January 1907 Alexander Fleming, David Lindsay and James Donnelly, three young men all around 20 years old, were killed in Philpstoun mine (Number 5) after a gas explosion. While a telegram was despatched to summon Dr Thom from Linlithgow, the men mounted a rescue effort and crawled over the fallen roof, discovering Fleming and Donnelly alive, but sadly not for long; efforts to apply artificial respiration failed to stave off the asphyxia caused by the 'after-damp'. Finding Lindsay took far longer – by now, the underground search party had also been joined by Archibald and Robert Crichton – but when they eventually located him, it was clear that he had been caught in the explosion itself. He was in the 'waste' – the area left after the shale in the stoops was extracted and a notorious collection point for gas. He was dead and given the extent of his injuries, it seemed likely that his lamp had been the very one to ignite the gas.

In reporting the accident on 1 February 1907, *The Courier* noted that 'it has been said of them by one who is in a position to speak with some authority, that 'there were not three better young fellows in the district of Philpstoun, where it is needless to say that the sad calamity has caused great consternation and sorrow'.'

The Courier also carried a report of an 'alarming fire at Philpstoun Oil Works' in June 1926, where the men saw flames 'coming from the scrubber oil pumphouse plant'. The men jumped to the firehose and extinguishers, thankfully bringing the blaze under control before it could reach the nearby petrol tanks.

Canaries were not the only beasts to be employed in the mine: the pit ponies played a vital role, and not just in pulling the hutches. Occasionally, the men would hand over a light pay packet to their wives at the end of the week, claiming that it was their turn to feed the cuddies. Many was the wife who recognised the word as slang for horses, so said little. Some of the more sensible women reprimanded their men for not having thought to save up their old bread and keep the precious money, or even turned up at the pithead with bags of scraps for the poor beasts. What these women failed to realise was that in fact 'cuddies' were the weighted hutches used to counterbalance the full hutches on the 'cuddie braes', or branch lines leading to the workings from the main haulage...

(Another local mining term from the turn of the 20th Century no doubt also provided room for misunderstanding: an 'Irishman' was a 'shot hole drilled almost vertically into the roof'.)

There were real ponies, of course – looked after by the pony drivers, the mine stable lads. A pony could pull several hutches full of shale at any one time and they varied in height depending on the size of the shale seam, Whitequarries having the tallest ponies because of the height of the faces. About a dozen ponies were stabled at the Dairy and the station for the Philpstoun mine and, like the men, they would walk down to work. (In the pit mines, the ponies were often lowered in nets fixed to the bottom of the cages that took the men down to the workings.) Some mines also had underground stables, but the animals were brought up to the surface regularly. When they were too old to work, they were put out to pasture until they died – a well-earned reward. Many of the lads took great pride in their charges and there were frequent regional competitions for the best turned out ponies.

Shale makes for cleaner workings than coal, being higher and not as damp. Neither was it cold underground, but a steady temperature night or day,

Pit Ponies
(photograph courtesy of BP)

whatever the season. Visibility was also good, as there were electric lights all along the main haulage.

That said, it was no paradise. The noise was perpetual. Surface water would constantly drip down and was guided into a pool or 'sump' from where it would be pumped out – a continuous process requiring a dedicated pump operator. Given that neither man nor pony came above ground during a shift, there was also a role for the other mine inhabitants: the rats.

Lunchtime down the mine was straightforward – you pulled out your tin piece box and cold tea, sat on a sleeper and ate; the term 'lunch break' had yet to be coined. (Oncostmen did have a set time, usually 10 to 10.30 during the day shift, so it made sense to try to tally with them). Niceties such as the washing of hands before eating were equally unknown, and not surprising since there were no washing facilities underground. There were also, of course, no toilet facilities in the mine (at one time they tried taking down pans and they were being used, but no-one would empty them) so the sanitary removal was performed admirably by the mine rats. The men would also throw them bits of sandwich. Man and rat working in harmony.

The company may have looked after its own, but it was no charity. In the earlier days there was no union, or at least none to speak of, and the company retained total power to hire and fire as it chose. Being ill meant not being paid. An injury sustained in the mine would lead to compensation, but nowhere near as much as the man could have earned had he been at work.

Further to the Workmens' Compensation Act of 1906, compensation was paid for injury and death. An injured man received half his normal wage, to a maximum of £1 a week, while dependants of a deceased worker would receive a lump sum to a maximum of £300. This prompted the oil companies to join insurance schemes and many workers also joined Friendly Societies such as the Rechabites or Foresters which would provide some additional financial support in times of disability. Claims were administered by the Sheriff Court: the 1911 records for Linlithgow show that the Court handled 50 claims from Philpstoun workers that year, allocating a total of £555.

The reality of compensation for the family should the worst possible situation arise – the death of their main breadwinner in the works – was that it was pitifully small. In just one example, Mrs Zena Watson's father died in Glendevon mine in February 1911, leaving a wife and three small children. The 'compensation' to his wife for the loss of her man was paid over to her on a canal bridge between Winchburgh and Niddry: £72, with no question of a pension. Trying to keep the rent paid and the children supported, she turned to the parish. The head of the parish relief fund gave her another one-off payment: a shilling. One shilling. Five pence. So she took in washing.

(If the man of the house died, the company did not evict his widow and family, but of course they had to keep paying the rent. As it could hardly be deducted at source any more, one of the company's employees – by the 1950s, Davie Walker – would come around to collect it once a week.)

The Lothians did not escape the depression. Local buyers were turning to cheaper oil sources, like Glasgow Corporation which was buying Russian oil products, and in March 1925 the Admiralty withdrew its Fuel Oil Contract from Scottish Oils, a devastating blow leading an independent Court of Enquiry to conclude that the Scottish shale-oil industry would never again work at a profit. Some 2,000 men were laid off during the 1920s as many works closed (although roughly half of them were re-employed under the spread-over scheme in the 1930s).

In 1925, Scottish Oils reduced ('broke') the remaining men's wages, the only way that they could see to keep the works open at all, prompting an all-out six-week strike called by the now quite active shale miners' union. Led by Walter Nellies, the union man for the underground workers, and Michael Hagan for the surface workers, a meeting was called at Bridgend School where they vowed to 'stay out until the grass grew over the pit pulleys'. A soup kitchen was set up in the hall and the soup made by local ladies like Mrs Ford with turnips and tatties supplied by the farmers. Some men, like Jimmy Flood, left for the coalfields in the East to collect money to support the strikers, reminiscent of the bands that used to come to play in Philpstoun to collect money when the Fife coalfields were on strike, but it all came to naught and the men returned to work.

In 1928 the Government helped to stem unemployment by establishing a tax preference exempting the domestic shale-oil industry from a newly-imposed motor fuel duty. However, the best of the shale had already been worked and competition from cheap foreign imports continued to grow. Many were the weddings that had to be postponed for years in this period.

Scottish Oils' decision to start processing crude oil from the Persian Gulf at its new refinery at Grangemouth in 1924 was another blow. Although the domestic industry kept afloat, diversifying into diesel fuel and new detergents, Philpstoun mine was to close in July 1931 with many of its workers being forced on to the dole. The men gradually found other jobs, some having to move to the coalfields for a couple of years before openings came up at Winchburgh, Whitequarries and Duddingston.

The site of the old Philpstoun mine was cleared in 1935 under the supervision of James Burns and became a playground for the local children (but make sure to wash your feet in the canal on the way home if you don't want a row for being up the bing...), only to come to life again briefly during the Second World War as an air-raid shelter.

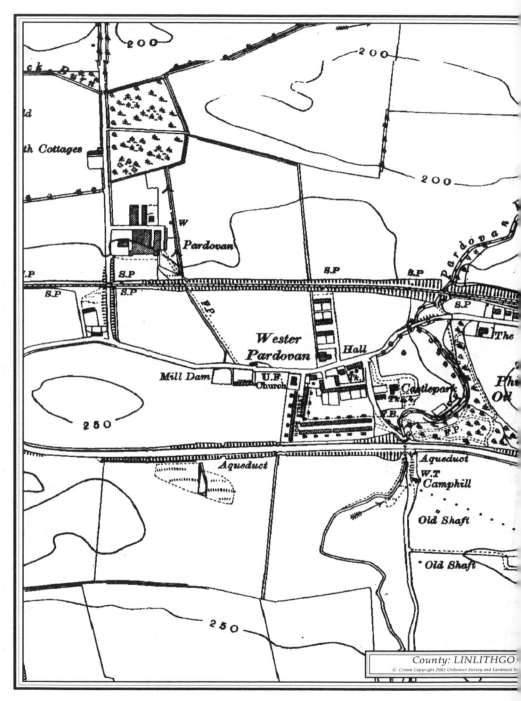

1922 Map

In an attempt to stay in business, and bolstered by the extended shale-oil preference from the Government, from 1932 the shale companies instituted a 'spread-over scheme' – three weeks on, one week off, for £2/10/- and 37/- from the dole respectively. This led to the re-employment of some 1,000 men, bringing the total workforce of the Linlithgowshire shale field to about 4,000 by 1935. (To supplement their families' tables in these times, some of the men reportedly liberated the occasional rabbit from the Hopetoun estates).

The full average weekly salary of £2/10/- for a faceman was quickly accounted for – and always but always handed straight to your wife or mother. There was the rent and light – 5/- and deducted at source, including 7d for the electric lighting – and £1 of Co-op 'cheques' for your messages from the vans (a hundred weight of coal being 1/6d). After the 5/- for your man's pocket, that left £1 for everything else.

This included the fee for the Linlithgow doctors like Cross, Candlish and Carter (who doubled as the dentists), which had risen to fourpence a week per worker by the 1930s. (The doctor would make home visits so long as you left word at the store that he was needed.) There was also a voluntary subscription of 2/6d a year for the (white) Linlithgow ambulance, and you could pay a penny a week for the Edinburgh infirmary and for the services of a nurse. Any medicine required was supplied for free.

Despite the doctors' money being stopped at source from the men's wages, there were no Scottish Oils medical facilities. The company did have a (blue) ambulance for anyone injured at the works which it would also allow to be used to take villagers to hospital, especially in the earliest days when there were epidemics of diphtheria and scarlet fever, and patients had to be taken to the Fever Hospital at Tippethill.

In all, working life was hard and there was a constant fear of redundancy. Losing your job meant losing your house and not feeding your family, so most thought themselves lucky to be employed, no matter what we may think of the conditions.

CHAPTER FIVE

The Land

PHILPSTOUN HAD, OF COURSE, originally been an agricultural community and the farms did not just disappear because the mines arrived. Fairniehill (formerly Easter Pardovan) thrived, as did the farm at Old Philpstoun. By the turn of the 20th Century the closest farm to the centre of the village – Pardovan – was a large operation run by John Clarke of Pardovan House, his lands extending up to Hopetoun and down to the Troughstone.

(Pardovan Estate was actually owned by the Duke of Hamilton and when the Estate was sold in the summer of 1920, Ross purchased the Pardovan feu of just over one acre which they had originally taken in 1917 with the intention of building houses as soon as the war was over. By 1925, they still hadn't built said houses but the Ross Lease Book does contain a rather forthright explanation for why they had made the purchase, to whit: 'it was not desirable that the feu should pass out of our hands into those of an outsider who might build in the heart of the village'.)

After the Great War the Board of Agriculture for Scotland began to buy up private farms and split them into small-holdings, with the intention of renting them to ex-servicemen. Following the death of Mr Clarke, his widow sold all of the farmland to the Government and kept only the house. It was on this land that the Holdings were created in 1931. (The farm at Old Philpstoun was not sold, belonging as it did to Hopetoun, and Geordie Walker also chose to keep Fairniehill.) Despite Governmental intentions, not many ex-servicemen actually wanted them, so many of the local families became the tenants.

The largest of the Holdings covered around 50 acres, the smallest ones 6 or 8. The tenants were housed in the existing ten farm workers' cottages from Pardovan farm or in new houses built for the Holdings, which were quite modern for the day – even boasting bathrooms. Tenants of new properties were granted a loan to cover their construction, although the building was actually carried out by contractors from the Department of Agriculture with bricks from Winchburgh brick works, brought to Pardovan by horses and carts from Cadgers' Bridge. The system was thus akin to a modern mortgage as they had 50 years to pay back the loan, although the original tenants could not let or sell the property: it could be handed down through the family but had to be returned

Tommy and Ena Hamilton
(photograph courtesy of T Hamilton)

to the Department if the tenants left. Second tenants would then just pay rent to the Department.

Not every man in Philpstoun worked for Scottish Oils therefore; some worked the land. Some ended up doing both – in the 1920s some of the farm workers, like Tommy Hamilton's ploughman father, found that they could make slightly more money at the works then they could in the fields so headed off to the Philpstoun mine. (A ploughman was estimated at the time to walk an average of 22 miles a day, so moving to the mines would not exactly be regarded as a hardship posting.) With the closing of that mine, however, Mr Hamilton took himself off to the dairy at Blackness before eventually coming back to the Pardovan Holdings. Some of the miners would also be seen turning out to help with the harvest when they came off shift.

For children growing up on the farms, life was just as hard as that of their mining family friends, although their chores were more likely to be hand milking the cows, working the horses or feeding the hens than washing up. Just as the village boys would automatically go to the mine, the Holdings boys left school to work at the farm: there was no real choice.

In the earliest decades of the century, much of the heavier farm work depended of course on the horses but, as industrious as these beasts were, they could not always be relied upon. In the snow, for example, they were little use, their feet sliding from under them, so in the worst winters they might not leave the stables for six weeks at a time. No horses meant little work could be done, so as soon as there was a break in the weather the farm workers would be out from sunrise to sunset trying to make up the time lost.

As well as providing homes and jobs for families such as the Hamiltons, Mansons and Blackleys, the Holdings were also, naturally, providers of milk to the village. Before the establishment of the Scottish Milk Marketing Board in 1932, farmers sold their milk to whoever would buy it. Thereafter, all produce could be sold to the SMMB, rather like a large co-operative, so the farmers knew that all of their milk would be taken every day, any excess being made into cheese or other dairy products.

The Mansons instead chose to retail their milk. From 1932 until well after the war, their cart would do the rounds of the village every day pulled by their horse Ramsay, later replaced by Dixie, with a large urn of fresh milk and a measuring jug, in competition with Broxburn Co-op's delivery service.

The Holdings also provided a few weeks of seasonal work for the village women. Once the crops were ready for reaping, the farmers would bring their carts, then tractors, to Philpstoun looking for workers. All the farms would help each other out with the harvest (including Fairniehill) but bringing in the potatoes alone could be a job for a month, so the extra labour was essential.

It was a two way street – the women needed the money and the farms needed the women.

The children safely off to school, a dozen or so women would climb into the farmer's cart, ready to earn 2/- an hour (in the 1930s, when a hundred-weight of potatoes sold for 7/6d and an extra 10/- a day went a long way) howking tatties. Each farm would provide a few days' work and then off they would all go, women and farm workers alike, to the next. The potatoes were sold to a tattie merchant from Bo'ness who came with his machine to dress (clean and sort) them before taking them to be sold, or turn the poor ones into swill.

The women would also help with the 'shawing' of the turnips: pull, top and tail and leave in rows wide enough for the cart to pass through the middle and load the turnips either side; and at the threshing mill.

So important was the bringing in of the harvest that the older children could even get a permit from school allowing them to help, earning 1/- an hour. The farmers were responsible for marking these permits, to ensure that it was the tatties and not the truancy that was the true reason for absence.

This wasn't new – for decades there had been special school holidays in October (exact dates depending on the harvest) so that the children could help in bringing in the tatties. On 15 September 1911 *The Courier* carried a summary of a debate about such holidays, noting that 'about this period of the year when the season for potato-lifting was on, the Board always found that the attendance of children at school became very irregular', and a week's holiday had been established 'apparently in order to preserve the record of attendance'. Noting that it was not so much a case of the farms having access to cheap labour as poorer parents needing the money, the authorities noted that 'if the children of poor parents earned say five shillings, it would help to get them boots for the winter months and in that way maintain the good attendance during the cold weather'. A means to a very laudable aim.

This traditional harvesting began to die out after the Second World War. Families had that wee bit more money so didn't need the extra shillings so much and biceps were being replaced by machines, so bit by bit the tattie farms in the area have disappeared.

There were other, albeit smaller, agricultural interests in the village. From March 1919 until at least April 1921, 4.25 acres of Castlepark's grounds were used by the Board of Agriculture for Scotland as a trial ground for testing new varieties of potatoes, originally for a rent of £5 per acre.

Some of the shaleworkers' families had a bit of land too. In 1933 the Department of Agriculture for Scotland launched a scheme to allocate small plots to families of the unemployed miners. A circular issued by the Department explained that the scheme was different from, and not in competition with, existing allotment schemes as the plots were intended for a much wider range of activities than would be possible on the latter – everything from raising potatoes to keeping poultry or rabbits. The rents varied from about 6d to 10d per acre per week although no rent was charged for the first season. The plot-holders could get all of the tools and seeds necessary from the Department, payable by weekly instalments.

At first there was some reluctance to take on the plots as the men thought that this would affect their unemployment benefits. However the Department made it clear that this was not the case and the scheme grew in popularity. Eight acres of Fairniehill land were taken over and turned into 19 plots of about half an acre each. Some were further sub-let so about 25 people in all worked them, growing potatoes, cauliflowers, sprouts, cabbage, leeks, turnips and other vegetables and fruit. Mrs Currie and Mrs Cosgrove also kept hens. They even gave their name to the track that leads down to Gateside road just beyond the canal bridge – the plot road.

There were also some individual arrangements. For example, George Gray of West Philpstoun was granted a lease by Ross for part of the old Wester Pardovan Farm land in 1924 for 'grazing purposes' and in 1934, Thomas Kilpatrick (of 57 Hope Street) took a lease from Ross of 3.163 acres of Avenue Park (almost opposite Castlepark, to the right of Pardovan Crescent). In 1945, William Kerr (of 45 Hope Street) took over the lease 'for cultivation and hen runs', providing another source of fresh produce, including rhubarb and eggs, for the villagers. The ground was sold to West Lothian County Council in 1948.

CHAPTER SIX

Women . . .

PHILPSTOUN'S WOMEN MAY NOT have been employed at the works, but they were far from idle. Keeping house and family was a full-time, and far from easy, job in itself.

Apart from the seasonal harvesting, there was no work for women in the village – meaning of course no *paid* work. While the boys headed for the mines or oil works, their sisters packed their bags and disappeared off into domestic service in response to adverts in the local papers.

Young girls who had never been away from home before, let alone in the big city, found themselves despatched on the 8.40 bus from Gateside on Sunday evening, the 'skivvies bus', to meet total strangers in far-flung places like Edinburgh or Dundee. One day they were schoolchildren but the next, at the ripe old age of 14 (or even younger), girls used only to country life would find themselves as house maids and companions to city folk, dressed in crisp starched uniforms and sleeping in garret rooms.

The positions varied. Mrs Watson started as a dormitory maid at a boys' college (the boys, naturally, were always up at the main college when the girls were in the house) then worked at the Edinburgh University Hospice. Mrs Philbin started off doing small jobs at Pardovan House while still at school, then moved to work with a doctor's family in Murrayfield before ending up as companion to the widow of the Moderator of the Church of Scotland. In all the story is much the same – parlour maid or lady's maid, they were still a long way from home.

The girls may not have been badly treated but no amount of rich upholstery can make up for missing your family and many is the tale of the lassies who ran back home no sooner than they arrived,

Martin and Katie Philbin
(photograph courtesy of K Philbin)

or were left, at their jobs. They might cry, they might be painfully homesick, but if they did turn up at home they would be sent straight back; there was just not enough money for them to stay.

Just like their brothers, the girls would send any money that they earned to their mothers, who would buy their clothes (including the uniforms they needed for work) and let them have enough back to cover the bus fare for the trips home: every second Sunday and their monthly 'weekends' off (Friday to Saturday). Locally placed girls could also sometimes come home on their half days (usually Wednesday) – those further away would just spend their free time taking a walk around the local park or catching up on their mending; there wasn't much else they could do with no money.

The girls would stay in service until they married, and that was usually to a local boy; they may have been working in the city but the men there were regarded as too 'fast-living', and not the sort of son-in-law of whom mother would approve. The body may have been in the city, but the heart remained in the village.

With most of the teenage girls only in the village on rare days, the local dances took on a great importance for lads and lasses alike. Before the building of the hall, a melodeon would play outside on the grass and later there would be dances or socials in the hall every month or so. The earliest of these dances, accompanied by a piano and a fiddle, would often go on all night, only ending about 5am to give the men time to get into their working clothes.

While they were not exactly chaperoned, it took a brave man to approach a girl at these events. (Grace Mushet well remembered the excitement of her first dance at the hall – tempered slightly by her six brothers watching her every move.) Most of the teenage girls also knew better than to be home later than 9, if they did not want a veritable brigade of relations, or worse still their father, turning out to meet them.

Some older girls would stay in the village to help their mothers with the family, or to raise the younger children if their mother had died, and with the endless round of cooking and cleaning – all, of course, by hand.

The washing was a full day in itself: filling the boiler with water in the outside wash-houses; stoking the fire to heat it up; washing the clothes in wooden tubs standing on solid stools and scrubbing them on wooden washing boards; re-filling the tub with clean water for rinsing; wringing them out by the manual wringers attached to the back of the stools; fetching and setting up the ropes and stretchers; and hanging them out to dry on the shared greens... all to watch them freeze solid in Philpstoun's not quite tropical climes.

Every family had its set washing days, so too bad if it rained – or snowed. There were pulleys in the house – pulled down by ropes from the ceiling – but

Kitchen Range
(photograph courtesy The Almond Valley Heritage Centre)

they were really only good for drying smaller items. Sheets were best dried on the green, and then put through the big mangle in the wash-house instead of being ironed by hand.

The cooking was originally done on open fires, part of the large ranges that needed almost constant black-leading with Zebo. As the only source of heat in the original houses (unless one counts the paraffin lamps) they almost always boasted a huge kettle so at least there was some warm water in the house.

Around the end of the Second World War, much to the delight of the women, they were replaced by tiled ranges with 2 hobs and paraffin stoves. (Shiny whistling kettles were usually found on top of the latter – which stayed shiny as these ones were never allowed anywhere near the mucky coal fire.) As well as using the hobs, the women could also cook on little extensions to the paraffin stoves that easily had room for two pans. Some families could even afford little metal ovens that sat on top of them. These small stoves often sat on the bath cover in the scullery, providing heat for that room too, and then in the 1950s the ultimate in appliances arrived: bottled gas cookers.

Food was not scarce, but plain and whatever it was, you never said no. Usual menus would be porridge (or sometimes eggs) for breakfast, sandwiches for lunch and Scotch broth, stovies, or tatties and mince for dinner. Fruit and vegetables also grew locally and most of the women would bake, griddle scones being a favourite

The only real variety might be on Sundays, when sometimes there would be a special lunch, like a 'swivel' on the fire (steak and onions), or for visitors when Mammy would buy 'tea bread' for a penny halfpenny, but heaven help a child foolish enough to touch it.

Cleaning the house was of course a daily,

Paraffin Stove
(photograph courtesy The Almond Valley Heritage Centre)

not weekly, occupation. The houses may not have been big but the women were generally very house-proud, vying with each other to have the cleanest curtains or most spotless doorstep. One of the benefits of working in a shale community was that the village was one of the first to have the new wonder-detergent produced at Pumpherston in the 1940s. (The war-time shortages of fat-based soaps had encouraged the company to experiment.) Originally known as 'Iranopol', the prosaically named 'By-prox' and its companion 'Comprox' were strong liquid soaps and extremely popular with housewives for cleaning the house and the dishes. Indeed, some of them still fondly remember By-prox as being 'streets ahead' of modern products.

The women would make their own 'clootie rugs' for the floor out of old clothing and canvas, some of them even with designs, remembered as being 'very practical'. They would also make curtains to cover the bed recesses and nets for the windows, although the heavy paper blinds were normally bought from the hardware vans.

Sewing and knitting took up a good deal of time of course, especially for a young mother with a growing family. There were also the jerseys, underwear and socks to be made for the men who had the coldest jobs outside, and special hand protectors and caps with pads sewn in for the men who would tip the hutches of hot spent shale with hands and forehead over the top of the bing.

If the weather was fine, the women would gather together outside their homes with their mending or knitting needles, settled on the buckets (the dustbins) made comfortable by well-stuffed cushions, allowing a healthy mix of work and gossip until their man's supper needed to be fixed or the children came home from school.

(The children, especially, the boys, were not always too impressed that the women got the prized places on the buckets and would come up with any number of tricks to get them off. One of the most ingenious was during the Second World War, when some of the lads discovered to their delight that peeries let off a wail that sounded just like an air-raid siren, a sure fire way to send the women running for the shelters and for the buckets to become vacant, albeit temporarily.)

No-one remembers real trouble in the village, but that is not to say that the odd cat-fight never broke out, with squabbles over rights to the drying green, the behaviour of (some else's) children or comparisons of their men's footballing prowess. However such battles never lasted for long: as soon as they came to the ears of Mr Crichton, the men would be called to Castlepark and told to keep their women under control, or lose their job – and thus their house. The women invariably made up.

Although women would give up work when they married, it was perfectly normal to take small jobs – like the harvesting – while the children were in school. The concept of the 'latch-key kid' was some decades away though, as your mother would always be home before you were, or you would know in which field she was working and you would go straight there and play until she was finished. As everyone needed the money everyone understood this, including the children who knew that mother's word was, quite simply, law. (By the 1950s women did sometimes have other jobs, like working in Linlithgow shops or as cooks in works' canteens. Some women, like Mary Savage, also walked down past Old Philpstoun to catch the bus to Queensferry to work in the distillery.)

Everyone, no matter what their station, was always there to help in times of need: that was simply what you did. The women would also rally to any local causes, flying the village flag of pride along the way.

For example, the Catholic women wanted to help to raise the £100 needed to put electric lighting into St Michael's RC Church in Linlithgow for the Golden Jubilee in 1938, so they took turns to hold whist drives in each other's houses (with the leftover food of course appearing in the man's piece box the next day). Mrs McKeon's famous knitted socks, which were already valued prizes in card games among the men, now also became raffle prizes, with Mrs Sweeney and Mrs McKeon going around every door in Philpstoun, Bridgend and Winchburgh selling tickets. No-one was going to say that the Philpstoun women hadn't done their bit.

During the war, all the women rallied for the Red Cross – knitted socks once again playing a starring role – and some filled the vacancies left by the soldiers, on the land or in Nobels factory in Linlithgow.

The women may not have gone out to work, but they were far from being considered 'inferior'. Their homes were well run, the children supported, the food made and the mending done - all with little more than pennies.

Home and family were priority number one. Some women were in the Women's Rural, others helped out with the Gala Day preparations, all were there to help out a neighbour – but family came first. The man's pit clothes would be laid out on the fender board to warm, as would his day clothes in time for his coming home, and his tea would be ready as soon as he was. While their men spent their leisure time playing sports or socialising up at the hall, the women would be at home, making up the pieces ready for their man's box the next morning, or preparing the half-time refreshments for the sportsmen, and watching the bairns; they only ever went up to the hall for a social.

As for feeling unappreciated, far from it; their work was essential, and they knew it.

Wedding guests in Philpstoun Hall
Martha McCluskey (Mary Savage's sister-in-law), Mary Savage (authors' mother/grandmother), Mary Cosgrove,
Elizabeth Duncan, Winnie Savage (Joe's wife), Hannah Cosgrove
(photograph (taken 22/7/1961): B Pattullo)

. . . and Children

IF ANYONE HAD EVER tried to tell the children of Philpstoun that they were deprived, they would not have been believed. It is hard to be envious when all of your pals have just the same as you and there is no mass media telling you otherwise.

All of the local children attended school, generally starting at 5 and finishing at 14, although it was possible to get a special exemption to leave earlier if they had passed their Labour Certificate (the Merit Certificate took longer). They would leave well versed in the 'three Rs' (special emphasis on composition, spelling and grammar), history and geography. There were also, of course, school sports for both boys and girls – football teams, netball teams, rounders and the like.

In the earliest days of the village, all of the children went to school together, walking up Gateside to Bridgend or over to Whitequarries (now Abercorn) schools, in their bare feet if the weather was fine[1].

At Bridgend School the Headmaster even taught Latin at the end of the 19th Century to the senior boys before the school day opened. All pupils also had to learn the Scottish Catechism by heart in the fourth standard (when they were about 11) – not a greatly enjoyed endeavour.

At about the same time, pony-drawn 'peep shows' would sometimes visit the schools, showing pictures of Edinburgh Castle or the Houses of Parliament through small mirrored viewers in the side of the carts for a small fee. Illusionists also came to entertain the children and a photographer would come every other year or so for the obligatory class shot. Annual school concerts doubled as the prize-givings, the books perhaps presented by the Chairman of the Linlithgow Parish School Board – our own Mr Archibald Crichton.

The children at Bridgend School came from Philpstoun, Bridgend, Burnside, Threemiletown, Kingscavil and the Red Rows; according to a report on the

---

[1] According to *Groomes Ordnance Gazetteer of Scotland c.1895*, the 'hamlet of Philpstoun, 2¹/₂ miles sw of Abercorn village', fell within the boundaries of the Parish of Abercorn. This was one of the oldest parishes in the country: indeed, the monastery of Aebercurning was mentioned by the Venerable Bede and it had a bishop as from the 7th Century. The boundary between the parishes of Abercorn and Linlithgow was the small burn just east of The Rows.

village water supply, there were already 440 pupils by January 1901. The oil company arranged for most of the teachers at this time to be brought in each day from Linlithgow.

The children generally mixed well, although the obvious rivalries existed between the boys, the road between the school and Bridgend farm providing the battleground, weapons of knotted scarves at the ready. Eye witness accounts claim that Philpstoun boys were usually the aggressors about 100 years ago; with the benefit of hindsight, the authors prefer the words 'high spirited'. In later years, teachers walking up Gateside to school were called upon to separate the lads on more than one occasion, or provide unwitting protection to more timid pupils.

This may have been before the days of superstars of the music or football scene but that doesn't mean that there were no national heroes. During the last years of the 19th Century, essential fashion items for the lads at Bridgend School included portrait buttons of the most celebrated officers in the Boer War. Collections pinned on jackets or caps made a fine show.

By the 1930s, Bridgend School had 6 classes with one teacher per class (Misses Walker, Thompson, Wilson, Chalmers and Ferguson and Mr Tully) and a tiered gallery, reminiscent of a lecture theatre. Not all of these teachers were liked, one in particular being infamous for reducing children to tears with her evil temper (although she did have a habit of giving each of her small pupils two sweeties on a Friday). The Headmaster took the last – or 'supplementary' – class.

Originally, of course, the school did not provide food, so the children would take with them their pieces and flasks of tea, keeping the latter warm on the school boiler. Later they were also given milk at the school (one teacher, thinking she was doing the children a good turn, would put it on the pipes to warm – of course, rendering it disgusting) and, in the 1930s, soup. While the children normally walked to school, there was – briefly – a bus during the 1930s, but as this cost a penny it was only for use in extreme circumstances like torrential rain.

Linlithgow Academy originally opened in 1894 and a growth of pupils led to the building of a new schoolhouse at the Low Port in 1900. All of the local schools under the Linlithgow Parish School Board were given a holiday that day and classes 4, 5 and 6 from Bridgend School joined the procession of local pupils to watch Lord Hopetoun lay the foundation stone. According to James Burns, a pupil at the time, the Bridgend Headmaster was very proud of his pupils that day who, in his eyes at least, marched, kept step and kept formation better than any other school.

The ceremony completed with a rousing rendition of 'All People that on

Bridgend School Photo (1930s)
Peter Mushet is fourth from the left on the second back row.
(photograph courtesy of P Mushet)

Earth do Dwell', the children went home full of tales of The Day that I Stood Next To Lord Hopetoun. (This would prove to be Lord Hopetoun's last public duty before he left to take up his post as Governor General of Australia. In October 1911 his statue, locally known as the 'Green Man' thanks to the weathering of the bronze, was unveiled at the Linlithgow Cross. It has now been moved to the Rose Gardens.)

At this time, most families could not afford to keep their children in secondary education – they needed the extra income. By the 1930s most children did stay on, moving schools at 11, but by then the Academy had a less than shining reputation so some of the Protestant parents started to send their children to Bo'ness Academy. Eventually Linlithgow Academy realised that they were very rarely sent the brighter children and complained. Henceforth pupils from its catchment area could only go to Bo'ness if they took a course not available at Linlithgow, such as secretarial classes.

The Sisters of Mercy had been providing some Catholic education in Linlithgow since the early 1880s and in 1889, lay teachers (Miss Sayers and Miss McEwan) took over in what became known as St Joseph's (the original name of the Catholic parish). There were some 150 pupils, split into two classes and lessons were held in the Baird Hall. By the time that the new school building was opened in the lea of St Michael's Catholic Church in 1892, the school had grown to 190 children.

Henceforth, Philpstoun's Catholic children trekked into Linlithgow every day, except for the very young for whom the 3½-mile walk each way was just too much. Most of these children thus stayed at Bridgend until they were considered big enough to get to St Joseph's, when they were about 7. Very rarely, on the coldest of days, the country children would be called to the front of the class and given a penny to take the train home to Philpstoun, but that penny had to be repaid by their parents the next day.

Far from regarding the walk to Linlithgow as a chore, the children made the most of their daily expeditions, eating berries and corn off the land as they ambled along the lanes, invariably arriving late. Miss Mary Cosgrove, later to become the first Catholic schoolteacher to come from the village (she taught at Bo'ness and later at Winchburgh), remembered well that despite their best efforts at hastily rubbing colour into their cheeks at the last moment to make it seem as if they had run the entire way, neither the famously strict Headmistress, Miss Hobin, nor her dreaded cane were convinced. (The children knew when she was in a bad mood it seems – every time she wore that navy dress with the red trim... The reason why St Joseph's favoured the cane, and not the traditional tawse, is unknown, but many an ex-pupil can confirm that until Miss Hobin retired in 1927, it did.)

Known as the 'country children', they brought in treacle or syrup sandwiches (unless they had passed them through the fence of the Linlithgow Poorhouse on the way, under the kind but misguided notion that the residents thereof did not have anything to eat) while the 'town children' went home for lunch. The country children also had the privilege of keeping their corked tin flasks of tea inside the guard of the schoolroom fire, ensuring a warm drink even if their pieces had long since disappeared. At the instigation of Miss Hobin's successor, Mr Hall, the school started to provide soup at lunchtime for a ha'penny a bowl and milk distribution followed as from February 1935 with the advent of the Government's free milk scheme.

Football was, of course, an important part of life for St Joseph's boys, and a good show they put on too – so good that in 1931 they won both the West Lothian County Shield and the five-a-side competition at the County School Sports event at Boghall.

Some of the older Catholic children also went to Linlithgow Academy (until the Catholic school St Mary's Senior Secondary opened in Bathgate in 1931), but were excused from religious instruction and school on Holy Days of Obligation, while the rest would stay at St Joseph's. Only the brightest children could aim to pass the Qualifying Examination for St Thomas's or Holy Cross in Edinburgh and then only if their parents could afford the extra cost.

When the buses started the children would of course go to school that way, but they – or rather their parents – had to pay the fare. It was only after the Second World War that the Council started providing bus passes for children who had to travel more than three miles to school.

Out of school, the children's first task was to attend to the chores set by their parents. Thereafter, they were rarely idle. Linlithgow District Council did not build the playground until 1947 (under an agreement with Scottish Oils that the Council had the 'privilege of erecting playground equipment on our Philpstoun recreation ground') so the bairns found different ways to amuse themselves. A firm favourite at the start of the 20th Century was to run bare-foot in the 'sheughs' during thunderstorms, and kick the can was always popular, the aim being to kick, run and hide in the closes before he who was 'het' could catch you.

The girls would often be seen skipping or bouncing balls to rhyming songs like '1, 2, 3 a leary'. A kind big brother or uncle might make you a cart with old pram wheels, or perhaps your Dad might get you a gird and kleek from the smithy at Old Philpstoun – a hoop which you could guide with a stick as you ran alongside. Marbles were also popular and the children were often seen hunting for five smooth pebbles so they could play chuckies, throwing up one pebble and racing gravity in trying to pick up the others before it landed.

Peevers (hopscotch) was another favourite, using a boot polish tin as it slid better than a stone, as were peeries, the whip and top that would let out a mighty screech. Any snowy winters would see all the wee'uns out sliding down the brae on shovels or tin trays – especially during the winter of 1947 when the village was snowed in for a week and they couldn't get to school. The odd bit of mischief crept in of course: Johnny Sweeney could have told you of the day they tied the Floods' and Kirkwoods' doors together so that as one opened, the other would shut... but in the main it was simple, innocent fun and the children would be at home long before it was dark.

The older boys might play football or cricket after school, or supplement the family income by taking on small jobs, all monies of course going straight to their mothers. (Or at least that was the theory... When Peter Mushet up at Bridgend was 14, he was on to a good thing. He would collect the coal and break the sticks for his Granny which earned him a tidy £1/2/6d a week, which he didn't think his Mum needed to know about, especially when there were so many football matches that he wanted to see. That was until his Mum got him a job helping out at the farm on Gateside – which only paid £1, and she knew about it. The half a crown that she would give him for his pocket seemed small recompense and that was the end of the football for a while.)

While well looked after, children were, after all, children, so they would always be sent out when anything important was discussed – like a neighbour announcing her pregnancy or the death of baby. The facts of life were gleaned from listening at keyholes, or in snippets handed down from older siblings or friends. (Passing on such knowledge bore its own risks: Grace Mushet well remembered having to do double chores under threat of being shopped to her mother for talking about 'such things' to her sister.)

Some families had wirelesses, many of them electric but some needing two accumulators (batteries), one to be taken away weekly to be charged while the other was used. However, these were strictly for use under adult supervision, and during the war only for the news, and well the children knew it. The risk of discovery for illicit listening was high, as the battery would only just last the week as it was.

In the early days, birthdays held no particular magic for most of the village children as birthday presents, or parties, simply did not exist. As for Christmas, while they were well versed in the lore of Santa Claus, shouting their wishes up the chimney or writing letters as the great day drew near, they knew not to expect more than an orange, an apple and a penny in their stocking, and maybe some small item of necessary clothing or a hanky – certainly nothing as useless as a toy.

In the opening years of the 20th Century the Sunday School and the 'normal' schools organised outings for all of the local children (regardless of denomination). They would head for the sea at Blackness or Hopetoun, or the park at Craigton, or even all the way to Ratho, in a horse-drawn canal boat or on the local farmers' hay carts, with the horses' manes and harnesses gaily decorated. Mothers, later the trip organisers, would prepare their little ones with a poke of food and a tin mug ('tinny') tied around their necks with ribbon to be sure it was not lost. Later, the children would be taken on bus and train outings.

(Two gentlemen in Bridgend also had a float and they would take both children and adults alike down to the sea at Blackness for a small fee. The only problem was that on the way back, the horse did not always make it up the brae so everyone would have to get off and push.)

Without a doubt the biggest event in the children's social calendar was the annual summer Gala Day. The first event was organised by the Philpstoun Oil Works Recreation Club ('PRC') on a Saturday afternoon in August 1917, bringing together the people of Philpstoun, Bridgend and Kingscavil on a field next to Champfleurie House. It was really a glorified sports' day, with races for boys, girls, married ladies, 'young ladies', men over 50 and boys three-legged,

1936 Gala Day Queen Janet Burns
(photograph courtesy of E Burns)

1939 Gala Day Queen Allison Reid
(photograph courtesy of A Jenkinson)

1949 Gala Day Queen Margaret Philbin
(photograph courtesy of K Philbin)

competitions for girls skipping ropes, air-gun shooting, 'washer pitching', a tug-of-war, a 100 yards sprint and a mile handicap and, of course, five-a-side football. There was even a pillow fight, a 'novelty race' and an egg and spoon race: shades of school sports days to come.

The Courier noted that 'although there was not much sunshine, the weather was dry' and a great day was had by all, culminating in Mrs Crichton presenting the prizes and the PRC giving a 'bag of eatables to each of 800 children of school age admitted to the field'. As this was before the time of the Philpstoun band, it was the Kingscavil Pipe Band that 'discoursed entertaining music during the proceedings' and as well as all of the above swings were erected to keep the children occupied. The day raised the princely sum of £10 which was handed over to the Red Cross.

By 1922 the event had moved up into Philpstoun, and forward into June, with the children marching after the pipe band down to the Hall Park to take part in the sports and watch the dancing exhibitions.

As from 1936 proceedings became rather more lavish with the coronation of Philpstoun's very own Queen. This honour went to the eldest daughter of the under-manager James Burns, Jenny (who was none too impressed to lose the School Board's perfect attendance record by having to take time off for the official photograph) with Isa Cowan and Jenny McCulloch as her ladies in waiting.

The Queen was attended by a chief lady in waiting, two further ladies in waiting and maids of honour. The Queen of the Fairies, usually in her early teens, had an entourage of fairies played by the 5 and 6 year-old girls, and the Queen of the Flowers brought along the flower girls, basically all of those who were too old to be fairies, carrying baskets of blooms.

Britannia was also present, complete with trident, helmet and shield, and there were pairs of bower girls to carry the flowered arches under which the Queen would pass as well as a pair of train-bearers. There was thus a place for every girl who wanted to be involved (although some could not be, if their parents could not afford the necessary pretty dress).

The boys were not quite so well represented. Apart from the Queen's Champion, a courtier and a herald, there were only two yeomen of the guard, a crown-bearer, a sceptre-bearer, Old Father Time and some pages.

Preparation started weeks in advance. Any child who wanted to be involved came up to the well-publicised meeting at the hall, signed up and then turned out for weekly rehearsals, where Miss Mary Cosgrove, Miss Wilson, Miss Stirton, Miss Thomson, Miss Pryde, Miss Catherine Burns et al would train them in their roles. All of the main parts were chosen by drawing names from a hat (although the queens always seemed to be tall, so there may have been a wee bit of engineering involved).

Gala Day 1949, Queen Margaret Philbin

James Hamilton, Nan Robertson, Ella Robertson, Alice Newbigging, Kathleen Walker, Dorothy Stein, Betty Robertson, Queen Margaret, Rena Walker, Eileen Grant, Jean Mallon, Jeanie Ballantyne

(photograph courtesy of T Hamilton)

On the day itself, those playing the main parts would gather at the hall – in later days a carriage, then a car was sent to fetch them – and the ceremonies would begin.

Led by the Dowager Queen, followed by the Queen Elect (in their own dresses – the style a closely guarded secret until the day itself – and the Queens' velvet, fur-trimmed cloaks), and accompanied by the pipe band, the procession would pass left out of the hall, around Castlepark, up and down The Rows which were lavishly decorated with flags and streamers and finally arrive through the guard of honour at a stage erected in the park. Any children not playing a part would join the back of the procession.

The Dowager Queen and her entourage (all in colours – again a secret, the girls just hoping that no-one else turned out in the same shade) would arrive first on the stage, where the regalia – crown, garland and sceptre – would be taken from her by her retinue and handed to the pages in the somewhat bleakly named 'de-coronation ceremony', ready for presentation, on cushions, to the new Queen. While the Dowager was presented with a bouquet, she recited a set speech wishing the new Queen luck, and was herself then addressed by Britannia. Jenny Burns, on passing her crown to Helen Mushet in 1937, was the first to avow that her tenure 'would linger in her memory'.

Gala Day 1949
Willie Hamilton, Harry Stein, Archie Davidson, James Hamilton (against the wall ? Russell)
(photograph courtesy of T Hamilton)

Philpstoun and District Gala Day

Under the auspices of Philpstoun Oil Works' Recreation Club

The Thirty-Sixth Annual

Children's Gala Day

CROWNING CEREMONY

and Children's Treat

To be held in THE HALL PARK, PHILPSTOUN

On SATURDAY, 7th JUNE, 1952

Children will assemble in the Avenue at 1.45 p.m. and will proceed therefrom around the village headed by West Calder Silver Band

PROGRAMME, PRICE SIXPENCE, which is given as a Donation to the Gala Day Funds, may bring you luck

P. Jameson & Co. Ltd. Linlithgow

1952 Gala Day Programme

SPORTS PROGRAMME

1. ADULT PILLOW FIGHT. Entry 6d each member
2. ADULT TUG-OF-WAR. Entry 1s each member
3. GIRLS' RACE, under 5 years
   BOYS' RACE, under 5 years
4. GIRLS' RACE, under 7 years
   BOYS' RACE, under 7 years
5. GIRLS' RACE, under 9 years
   BOYS' RACE, under 9 years
6. GIRLS' THREE-LEGGED RACE, under 10 years
   BOYS' THREE-LEGGED RACE, under 10 years
7. GIRLS' RACE, under 11 years
   BOYS' RACE, under 11 years
8. GIRLS' RACE, under 13 years
   BOYS' RACE, under 13 years
9. GIRLS' RACE, under 15 years
   BOYS' RACE, under 15 years
10. GIRLS' THREE-LEGGED RACE, under 15 years
    BOYS' THREE-LEGGED RACE, under 15 years
11. GIRLS' EGG-AND-SPOON RACE, under 15 years
12. BOYS' OBSTACLE RACE, under 15 years
13. GIRLS' RACE, over 15 years, if still at school
    BOYS' RACE, over 15 years, if still at school
14. GIRLS' SACK RACE, under 15 years
    BOYS' SACK RACE, under 15 years
15. GIRLS' PICK-A-BACK RACE under 15 years
16. BOYS' PILLOW FIGHT, under 15 years
17. GIRLS' NOVELTY RACE under 15 years
    BOYS' NOVELTY RACE, under 15 years
18. MIXED RELAY RACE, under 15 years
19. BAND RACE
20. BOYS' TUG-OF-WAR, under 15 years
21. BOYS' HALF-MILE RACE, 11 to 15 years
22. MARRIED MEN'S RACE
23. MARRIED WOMEN'S RACE
24. YOUNG WOMEN'S RACE
25. YOUNG MEN'S RACE
26. SLOW BICYCLE RACE
27. BOYS' FIVE-A-SIDE FOOTBALL, under 15 years
28. FIVE-A-SIDE FOOTBALL (ADULTS). Ties to be played on the Friday night and Final on Saturday. Adult Entry. 5s per team.

The above programme is subject to alteration by the Committee.

Words by Janet Savage Philipstoun   "HAIL! PHILPSTOUN'S QUEEN"   Music by R. S. Chisum Armadale

The butterflies salute her grace
With lightly flutt'ring wing,
The birds in every woodland place
Her queenly praises sing.
As bees the gladsome tidings spread
O'er hill and valley green,
Each blossom bows its comely head
In homage to our Queen.
    Chorus: Hail, etc.

May fairies e'er keep her bower
Secure from all mischance,
And fill each carefree hour
With laughter, song and dance.
May countless years strew her way
And ne'er a thorn be seen;
May life be one long gala Day
For Philipstoun's radiant Queen,
    Chorus: Hail, etc.

De-Coronation Ceremony

At 2.30 p.m. in the HALL PARK

Dowager Queen — HELEN STEIN

Chief Lady-in-Waiting	Rena Manson
Ladies-in-Waiting	Zena Watson, Barbara Savage
Maids of Honour	Margaret Scott, Ella Simpson, Mabel Hamilton
Courtier	George Stirton
Britannia	Jean Clark
Father Time	Billy Watson

Coronation Ceremony

To follow De-Coronation Ceremony in the HALL PARK

The Crowning Ceremony will be performed by
MRS. CRICHTON of Castlepark

HER MAJESTY'S COURT
Queen — AGNES MEIKLE

Chief Lady-in-Waiting	Hazel Simpson
Ladies-in-Waiting	Frances Currie, Margaret Davidson
Maids of Honour	Janet Headridge, Jean Ramsay
Queen of Flowers	Eileen Grant
Queen of Fairies	Margaret Paterson
Queen's Champion	Ian Sweeney
Queen's Herald	Tom Robertson
Crown-bearer	Duncan Munro
Sceptre-bearer	Alex. Currie
Pages	Jim Kerr, Allan Muir
Yeomen of the Guard	George Stewart, Tom Kilpatrick

The Dowager left the stage and heralded by a bugle call, the new Queen arrived with her escort (all in white) and took her place on the throne. After her Champion threw down his gauntlet, unsheathed his sword and declared that 'if anyone shall deny the Queen's title to the throne, I am here, ready and willing, to defend her in single combat', the new Queen was crowned by Mrs Crichton, to much bowing, curtseying and further speech-making. She was then given a small gift – often a watch – and the 'Queen of Hearts' was serenaded with 'Hail Philpstoun's Queen', the Gala Day Song (music by Richard Neilson, words by mine clerk and part-time violinist, Joe Savage):

Now mirth and gladness fill the air and all the world is gay
The fairies' wands have banished care from this our royal day
A lark trills out its music sweet, the sun shines on the scene
As we true loyal subjects meet to honour Philpstoun's Queen

Chorus: Hail Philpstoun's Queen, fairest of the fair
Happy be your reign with joy beyond compare

The butterflies salute her grace with lightly flutt'ring wing
The birds in every woodland place her queenly praises sing
As bees the gladsome tidings spread o'er hill and valley green
Each blossom bows its comely head in homage to our Queen   *(Chorus)*

May fairies ever keep her bower secure from all mischance
And fill each merry, carefree hour with laughter, song and dance
May countless roses strew her way and ne'er a thorn be seen
May life be one long Gala Day for Philpstoun's radiant Queen *(Chorus)*

Following a further round of speeches, cheers and the National Anthem, all the children were given a white paper bag of cakes and then ran off to play in the visiting fairground, ride the merry-go-rounds, watch the dancing exhibitions and join in the sports. (The platform party, being rather more elegant, had tea in the hall.) At the end of the day, the Gala Day Committee would gather in their props to be stored in the hall ready for next year while the adults joined in the Gala Dance and the children fell into bed dreaming of fairies and first prizes.

Even the war did not stop the Gala Day. There may have been no queens but the villagers still processed down to a field at the Holdings (the playing field having been cultivated) for a sports day. After the war the full proceedings returned, with Margaret Philbin in the role of the first Queen in 1949 under an arch made by Johnny Sweeney. Even though there was not always a queen thereafter (notably in 1953, when it seems that another Queen's coronation took precedence) the event was to continue into the 1960s, including the year in the 1940s that it was a total wash-out so the Committee just bundled all of the children on to the bus and took them to the zoo.

Thanks to the wonders of ciné photography, and a camera owned by Mr Keddie, two of the post-war Gala Days were filmed. Andrew Gault used to bring the reels up to Philpstoun sometimes to show in the hall and now, thanks to Miss Betty Burns, they have been transferred on to video cassette and placed in the safe-keeping of the West Lothian central library.

1951 Gala Day, Queen Helen Stein
Nan Blackley, Mabel Hamilton, Nita Connor, Jim Currie, Dowager Queen Elizabeth Brown, Rena Manson, Margaret Scott, Jim Kerr, Ella Simpson, Betty Robertson, Eddie Ward, George Stirton
(photograph courtesy of T Hamilton)

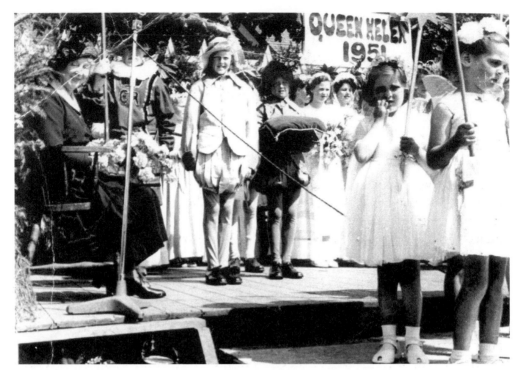

1951 Gala Day
Mrs Crichton, Tom Kilpatrick, Billy Watson, Nan Blackley, Nita Connor, Myra Hamilton, Jean Robertson

(photograph courtesy of T Hamilton)

CHAPTER EIGHT

After Working Hours

ALL WHO REMEMBER THE old village say it was a happy place, a true community where everyone looked out for his neighbour. Time and again those interviewed for this work commented that if you were ill, they would all be there for you: men and management might not mix socially but in times of need all pulled together. As noted by Miss Mary Cosgrove, 'there was not even one court case in all the time of [the village's] existence'.

As for locking their houses, well they had keys right enough, and the door might be locked, but the key would be hung from a nail next to the door, outside, in full view of everyone. Perhaps it was the principle of the thing. There was nothing unusual about leaving the door open all night in the summer – after all, what could happen?

As was the way all over the country at the time, social station and careers were to a certain level dictated by religion. The first Irishmen (the Catholics) who arrived usually had the dirtiest jobs, at the retorts or the bings, but then they generally came from far worse conditions with little, if any, education. On the other hand the men from Wanlockhead were well-read, well-educated and well-respected.

It was only in the 'second generation' that the gap began to close between Scottish Protestant and Irish Catholic, although some impressions, once rooted, take time to change. The tradesmen, office staff and management were without exception Protestant – originally under a deliberate management policy not to place Catholics in such positions. Indeed, in the entire history of the Philpstoun works only one Catholic ever worked in the office – Joe Savage – and he was never allowed to progress much beyond clerk.

Pardovan Church served as a focal point for the village, a good three quarters of the residents being Protestant, with two well-attended services on Sunday as well, of course, as the Sunday school. Bridgend School faithfully turned out excellent singers so the choir was consistently popular with participants and audiences alike. The lack of a church hall did not prevent the Women's Guild teas or other socials; the wooden pews were just pushed back to make room.

There was no Catholic church in the immediate area, but this was hardly surprising; prior to the nascence of the shale industry there were very few

Catholics around. It was the incoming Irish workers who would permanently change the religious make-up of the region, with Linlithgow getting its first resident Catholic priest in almost three centuries when Fr Andrew Smith began to say Mass at Spence's Tannery, later moving to other temporary venues in the Baird Hall, Green Park and Bridgend School before the foundation stone for St Michael's Catholic Church in Linlithgow was laid in 1887.

The church was eventually opened in 1893 (although occasional Masses were still said in Bridgend School several decades later) so while the Protestants attended Pardovan Church, the Catholics from Philpstoun joined other local villagers in the 3½-mile walk to Mass with the old folk being taken in Gardie Davies' horse and cart. Parents of small children would take it in turns to stay at home with them and attend different Masses.

Later, a bus came to take the Philpstoun people into Mass and when Pardovan stopped being a working church, two buses would come at the same time on Sunday mornings: one for the chapel and one to take the Protestants up to church in Kingscavil. While it is true that in the early days Catholic and Protestant did not really mix, later there was no such division, people instead simply graduating to natural friends, wherever they spent their Sunday mornings.

Funerals were usually organised in the afternoons so that the men on day shift could attend. Catholic families would hold wakes with people – usually at least one representative of every Catholic family – gathering to say the rosary at midnight every night between the death and funeral. If the death had been at home, the body would be laid in the bed and a sheet nailed around the bed recess until time for the funeral, and it would never be left: there would always be someone in the house.

On the day of the funeral, the coffin would be placed on the hearse which all the village men would follow to the main road. Any men going to the funeral itself would board a bus hired by the family to take them to Linlithgow Cemetery.

Everyone in the village worked hard, but they had their time for play as well. In the first days of the mine, local winter pastimes included skating and curling on Philpstoun Loch – a marshy expanse clearly marked on the older maps towards Fawnspark Farm but which had already disappeared under the Philpstoun bing by the time that the Ordnance Survey drew up its 1897 map of the area. That curling and skating were introduced at all to Philpstoun was down to the first under-manager, Mr Gilchrist, who came from Wanlockhead. Needing workers for the shale mines, he asked some men from his hometown to come to Philpstoun, which they did – complete with their curling stones and skates.

When the Loch disappeared they played, and skated, on the canal, lighting the ice with their pit lamps on their caps. Some of the lads would also play a sort of ice hockey, using a piece of wood as the puck. Indeed so popular was skating that it was not unknown to skate all the way to Linlithgow on the canal.

The early Irish workers brought a game hitherto unseen in the area, basically seeing who could throw iron balls the furthest and straightest. One of their favourite throwing sites was on the Main Road, east towards Winchburgh after turning left out of Gateside. Another popular pastime in the early village was quoits, each one weighing 4 or 5 lbs and thrown about 25 yards at a pin sunk in the ground. The original playing ground was out towards Philpstoun Mill and later there was one up Gateside. Men from Philpstoun, Bridgend and Kingscavil played (one of the most popular clubs went by the evocative name of The Sardines) in the County League until the last quoiting green closed in the late 1920s.

Running was also popular and some of the lads carried off a number of honours at the New Year and Christmas races at Powderhall in Edinburgh, including two ten-mile 'Marathon Handicaps', two New Year mile races and one two-mile race. Pitch and toss was, and stayed, popular round the back of The Rows.

There were also travelling magic lantern lecturers that would set up in the church or the old hall and concert parties would come in from Broxburn, Bathgate and Bo'ness, with elocutionists and singers who often seemed to specialise in the old Jacobite tunes. For the theatre proper, those that could afford the ticket would walk to the Victoria Hall in Linlithgow or go up to the Empire Theatre in Edinburgh on Saturdays, coming home on the popular 10.10pm train. Linlithgow also had the nearest cinema.

The centre of the village's social life was of course the village hall, at first the old farm building left over from Wester Pardovan at the Dairy and as from 1891, the new recreation hall (at this time, apparently just a room) provided by Ross. The opening of this facility was marked with a concert in Pardovan Church on 27 February 1891, which was written up in *The Courier* on 14 March:

> *A.H. Crichton Esq, JP, manager of the works, presided, and in his opening remarks referred to the institution of the Draughts Club over a year ago, and congratulated the members on their past success and the enterprise which had prompted them to extend the usefulness of their club by seeking in their new recreation room to make provision for the enjoyment of every form of indoor recreation and amusement. He expressed the hope that the club might be taken full advantage of by the people of the village and their neighbours, and go on with enlarged membership and increasing success in the future.*

The article details the programme of readings and songs, including performers from Linlithgow, Hopetoun, Edinburgh, Kirkliston and – of course – Philpstoun itself. (Peter Lockhart reportedly gave a 'highly appreciated' rendition of 'the sea is England's glory' but the 'special feature of the entertainment was Mr G Simpson, Philpstoun, in his humorous Scotch story, 'Peggy Kettle-poker' which fairly brought down the house'.)

Work on the Institute, or new village hall and recreation rooms, was first started in 1906, the men being docked a penny a week to pay first for the building, then its upkeep. It was completed in 1917 (although it was in service well before then). With its large functions room, billiards room and reading room it provided the perfect venue for the men to relax after work.

The old hall continued to be used: there were even Gospel meetings (for the Brethren) held there before and after the First World War, which had such an effect on some of the local lads that they became full-time preachers, some emigrating to the USA as 'Tramp Preachers', spreading the Word wherever they went. The old hall also continued to provide the venue for carpet bowls.

Although there was no strict rule preventing it, women did not usually go into the hall except for specific meetings, socials or dances. Boys would not go until they started work. A library was opened in the reading room at the hall on 26 October 1933, a branch of the County Circulating Library, with Henry Hogg as librarian. The reading room was also stocked with newspapers, periodicals and magazines financed through a kitty into which the men paid a penny or two a week.

Along with the hall came the Hall Committee. Philpstoun Recreation Club

Philpstoun Village Recreation Hall
(photograph courtesy of BP)

('PRC') was based at the hall and was, of course, run by Ross, then Scottish Oils, originally with Mr Crichton as President, John Muir as Vice-President and Matthew Crombie as Secretary and Treasurer. (Later Mr Calder (the manager of the local mines) took over as Vice Chair.) The annual subscription was 7/6d.

Under the Central Committee were a number of sub-committees for entertainments (originally chaired by Archibald Crichton), quoiting, billiards and the 'ambulance committee' (which ran first aid courses before the Great War). The reading room got its own committee in 1912 – with Archibald Crichton proposing that it should be given £5 to £10 a year to spend on 'good literature'.

The Central Committee could, and did, suspend members from using the hall for any misconduct. For example, the minute book held at the Blackburn Library cites several cases of suspension for disreputable behaviour and even a case where three men were expelled from the hall (in April 1913) until they owned up as to which one had damaged the cloth of the billiard table. The PRC also had a piano which they would rent out for various village events.

There were frequent dances and socials organised in the hall, around one a month, with music provided by local bands, accordion players and fiddlers. Anyone who wanted to organise an event could do so, as long as the Hall Committee agreed, and anyone who wanted to go could go, as long as they could afford the tickets.

There were events run like this by the tennis club, the bowling club, the angling club or the doo club (hence the wonderfully named 'doo dance'). For socials, all the women would pitch in for the food. One of the best attended was the annual social and prize-giving for the bowls and tennis clubs where there was a meal, a concert and then a dance.

The hall also hosted local concerts and variety shows, including frequent fundraising events during both wars for the Red Cross and servicemen's charities. Woe-betide any man that took a fit of the giggles though – one look from Mr Crichton was more than sufficient for propriety to return. Over the years the hall also housed meetings of the Women's Rural (once a month), a Boys' Club, a Girls' Club (that would put on concerts during the Second World War), a drama club (with scenery being made at the works thanks to Mr Keddie) and 'old time dancing' classes in the 1950s, as well as countless wedding receptions. In 1937 the tennis club even tried to persuade the Hall Committee to let them run a badminton club there during the winter, but the Committee thought that 'the hall was unsuitable for this purpose'.

(By 1954, the honorary President of the Hall Committee was Mr Keddie. According to the programme for the 1954 Testimonial to Mr Crichton, the Committee included: Jimmy Muir, Willy Currie, Dick Neilson, Johnny Ward, David Munro, Adam Manson, Davie Walker, George Hume, John Orr, Dick

Villagers outside The Hall

Standing: Mrs Kilpatrick, Mrs Paterson, James Laurie, Mr Paterson, Mr Paterson, Dave Munro, Mrs Brown, Mr Brown, Mr Kilpatrick, Mrs Kerr, Mrs Ford, Jock Ford, Mrs Duncan, Mrs McMahon, Tom Hardy, Mrs Gilchrist, Mrs Noble

Sitting: Kate Stein, Mrs Kerr, Mrs Orr, Mrs McLoughlin, Mrs Stirton, Mrs Paterson, Mrs Manson, Mrs Todd, Mrs Clark, Mrs Grant

(photograph courtesy of L Hamilton)

McKenna (who used to lodge with Mrs Duncan), Dick Grant, William (Coby) Watson, John Burns, A McKenzie, J Cameron, J Wishart, D Ramsay and A Orr.)

No mining village was complete without a football team, and Philpstoun Daisy was as good as any, boasting players like Andrew Harvey and Jimmy Savage (who was also a fully qualified referee for the Scottish Junior League) and David 'Berry' Sutherland who went on to play professionally with Airdrieonians in the Scottish First League. This was actually the senior team but by the early 1920s, the junior team, Castlepark Thistle (named, obviously, after the big thistle in front of Mr Crichton's house), was much the stronger: henceforth, they were Philpstoun's main team, although they drew players from all over, including Broxburn, Kingscavil and Linlithgow.

Although the team had been around for some time before the PRC got involved, in 1913 the Committee decided to see if there was sufficient support for an official team. On 25 November a special meeting was held in the hall, proposing that a club be established with members paying one shilling per year, the members to keep their own strip and the PRC to cover the rent of the field and to provide the balls. The 'large attendance' readily agreed to the proposal and voted in the football committee: Messrs T Muir, J Burns, James Kerr, T McGechie, R McCulloch, R Ritchie, R Paris, P Callighan, W Watson, G Brown and John Kerr.

The other villages were not quite as impressed. At the following meeting on 15 December, William Orr came to represent the Bridgend FC and told the PRC that his men 'were not agreeable to pay 1/- per member p.a. for football' – before then it had been free. After some persuasion, the 45 members of the Kingscavil club and the 20 Bridgend members fell into line.

Castlepark Thistle had a black and gold strip and used part of the old hall up the Dairy as the football hall and stripping box. The original pitch was the other side of the station, opposite the brick works and was a popular ground for local cup ties to be played on neutral territory – again, it has long since disappeared under the bing.

In about 1904, they moved to a pitch towards Fawnspark and later, when this too fell victim to the encroaching bing, to the rather less than flat area that is still used today (it wasn't levelled properly until after the Second World War). This pitch led to one of the team's greatest legends: the day that Mick Savage kicked a ball from Philpstoun to Stirling (courtesy of it landing in a wagon on a passing train). Part of this ground was bought by Ross from the Duke of Hamilton when he sold the Pardovan Estate in 1920, the rest from the trustees of John Clarke in 1938.

Between the wars the club went from strength to strength. A report from *The Courier* dated 25 August 1933 is the perfect example, describing how Castlepark Thistle opened the season with a 7:0 win over Douglas Wanderers

Castlepark Football Team (1939/40)

Front: Archibald ('Baldy') Orr, Davey Grant, James Boyle, ? Byrne, Dick Meikle, ??, Mick Coleman, Dick McKenna
Middle: 'Captain' Henderson, ??, Alan Kent, Jimmy Muir, Gus Plumb (future Hibs player), Jim Allen, ??, ??, Matt Mc Kelvie, John Sweeney
Back: Bert Keddie, Will Stirton, ??, Mr Crichton, George Orr (referee), James Caulfield
(photograph courtesy of E Sweeney)

(Cutler, Cosgrove, Russell, Mallon and Black (3)). Under Johnny Sweeney's management they won several cups in the West Lothian Amateur District League – they took home four separate trophies in the 1939-1940 season. They disbanded during the war but soon came back to form thereafter, even making it to the final of the Scottish Junior FA Cup at Hampden Park on 30 April 1949 (but the team lost through an own goal).

A number of the local lads went on to play in the professional leagues, like Gus Plumb and Bill Bruce who went on to Hibernian and George Sutherland who played with Partick Thistle. Later, Colin Stein would also join Hibernian, then Rangers, and he also played for the national team, while his brother Robert played for Raith, Montrose and East Stirling and another brother Eric was a Youth International.

Castlepark Football Team
Sitting: ? McKenna, Jimmy Coleman, Bert Muir, Jimmy Boyle, Tom Watson
Standing: Johnny Sweeney, Mick Green, Alan Kent, Jimmy Ward, ??, Jimmy Stirton,
Gib Manson, Adam Manson
(photograph courtesy of E Sweeney)

There was also a cricket club, which used to play out beyond Old Philpstoun at Philpstoun House. Exactly when they started is unclear, but it was likely around the start of the 20th Century. At the beginning there were few good players so the team relied on the men from the Hopetoun staff – except when Philpstoun was invited to play friendlies against the Estate including the young Hope sons, on the lawn up in front of Hopetoun House.

(The future eighth Earl of Hopetoun, Marquess of Linlithgow and Viceroy of India enjoyed cricket so much that he replaced the Hopetoun polo park with a cricket ground and pavilion and hired professional players. At one match when Philpstoun had gone up to play, one of the professionals visited them first in the dressing room and suggested that they might like to let the Marquess, who was captaining the Hopetoun side that day, make a few runs. Like true good sports, they readily agreed, only to find that they could not then get him out.)

That the original team was not too strong was partly due to the rather advanced age of most of their players. However, younger players started to show an interest and the Burnside and Threemiletown lads instituted regular practice sessions on the field that would later be the site of the Burnside post office, often to be accompanied by the best fielder and lost ball finder in the area, James Burns' father's dog, Logan.

Greatly helped by the strength of the Burnside players, the Philpstoun Cricket Club went on to win the West Lothian League Trophy in 1904 and again in 1911, beating Broxburn 158 to 54 in the deciding game at Fauldhouse with a team captained by Mr Irving (players including James Burns, Frank Semple, Mr McCubbin, James Gentleman, D McKenzie, B Nimmo, W Brown, D Brown, A Fleming, and William Brown – not one of whom actually came from Philpstoun itself). Before the Great War there was a County League of teams from Broxburn, Bathgate, Addiewell, Pumpherston, Armadale and Philpstoun playing against each other on Saturday afternoons, with a cup presented by Hopetoun.

During the Great War the games of course stopped, although one friendly with Broxburn at the Tarbert Asylum cricket ground during the war years would lead to several games between Philpstoun and Tarbert later. After the war the PCC played home and away matches for several seasons against a team of Indian students from Edinburgh University, which they usually won. One of their most memorable matches was when the students were joined by the famous Indian player Nazir Ali (who later went on to play in test matches against England). The Indian team arrived at Philpstoun by train with a great following (so much so that the locals had to send out for more food for their guests) but still lost. How things change.

The team drew good support from the village. As it did not come under the PRC, the men would go down to tend the grounds themselves and the women, like Nell Stein and Peggy Gault, would walk up from the village at half time with sandwiches and tea for the players. The original pavilion was destroyed by a falling tree during a storm but Hopetoun generously helped with funding for a replacement. The club was a member of the Scottish Cricket Union and had some excellent players, including James Fleming who went on to play for the Carlton Club in Edinburgh and for the national team and the County player James Newton. The popularity of the ground is evidenced by the fact that it was at Philpstoun that the West Lothian County Cricket Association, formed in August 1928, played its first match – against Stirling County on 29 May 1929.

The PCC remained popular until the Philpstoun works closed in 1931 when the situation of the men was so tenuous that they folded, selling their equipment and pavilion and donating their roller to the County Cricket Club. The left over funds were given to the PRC.

Although carpet bowls had been a favourite since well before the Great War it was not until 1922 that Scottish Oils built the bowling green (an idea originally proposed by the Hall's Central Committee in October 1913 but to a non-receptive audience). Bowling quickly became one of the most popular sports in the village. The men could either buy their own bowls or use the club's, stamped 'PRC'. The green was opened for the season by the pipe band and a local dignitary (Bob Crichton still has the dedicated Wonder Book of Empire to prove that the task fell to him in April 1934) and the championship was fiercely contested, the first ever champion being a Bridgend man, James Jamieson, in 1923.

The winning clubs from the county played off to enter County and Scottish Championships, held at venues like Queens Park in Glasgow or over in Ayr. The Philpstoun club once won the Hopetoun Cup, given to the club that sent out the best rink in the county and James Swan and John Neilson made a county record by winning the County Pairs together two years in succession. Philpstoun even carried off the Fraser Cup one year, despite several of their best players being absent.

The champions' board in the bowling pavilion names the winners from 1923 to 1963, Coby Watson (winner of the County Championship in 1937) being mentioned many a time, rivalling with William Allan. The club also participated in a number of exchange trips with miners from Wales over many years.

In 1930 Scottish Oils built two clay tennis courts in Philpstoun, with a small pavilion, which opened on 3 May. There had already been tennis courts at Burnside for some time and a very popular wee club that was too, but it did not benefit from Scottish Oils support like its Philpstoun neighbour so the maintenance was all down to the members. The Burnside club folded after the Second World War.

The Philpstoun club, however, seemed set for success – one year the tennis team was even the proud winner of the Bryson Scottish Oils trophy. The club remained open, and active, throughout the Second World War and invitations were issued to the soldiers stationed at the Merrylees camp to play at the club for

Mr Robert Crichton with Welsh Visitors
(photograph courtesy of Bob Crichton)

free. However, tennis was not as popular with The Rows folk and was mainly a sport for The Avenue (and Castlepark – Bobby Crichton being a keen player), no doubt because of the expense of the equipment, and eventually they began to take membership from further afield – Linlithgow, Bo'ness, Winchburgh and so forth.

When Scottish Oils closed, the tennis club rapidly followed as the committee could not persuade the members to pay the fee that would be needed for upkeep now that they had no subsidisation. The bowling green and tennis club were both sold to the Linlithgow District Council on 1 July 1963.

Ross, and later Scottish Oils, certainly provided some excellent sports and leisure facilities for their men. However, one thing that Messrs Crichton (father and son) would not allow was alcohol: the whole of Philpstoun, including the hall, was dry. No alcohol could be taken in at all, let alone sold. Robert Crichton ran all of the villages of Scottish Oils, including those as far afield as Pumpherston and Grangemouth, in the same way (although there was an anomalous 'licensed house' at Kingscavil). The bar in the bowling pavilion did not appear until many years after he died.

(This was far from unusual: in general, the oil companies did not approve of such indulgence. The reasons varied from the moral to the practical – a drunken worker generally not being the most productive worker.)

Perhaps it was better that Mr Crichton never knew of the occasional bottle lurking in a kitchen cupboard or cooling in the Hall's toilet cisterns during dances. What he would have thought if he had known that many of the men, and some of the women (even Mrs Keddie!), would bet on the horses (thanks to Mr Kerr, Frank Gartland and the omnipresent Johnny Sweeney and their wee meetings at the Duddingston Arms...) defies the imagination. Or that there was often a look-out posted in the Hall window to warn the dominoes players of Mr Crichton's approach so that stakes could be swiftly swept off tables into pockets. Then again, perhaps there was much that he did know but chose not to see: who can say.

Mr Crichton did not go so far as to ban the men from having a drink. The Blackness Inn was a favourite with the Philpstoun boys as was the Duddingston Arms, the perfect venue for a quick pint between coming off shift and heading home. The 5 o'clock train up to Linlithgow on a Saturday afternoon didn't just take the women in for the messages but the men in to the pubs too. The train home that arrived at Philpstoun at about 8.30 always bore a number of merry miners, and thus was always met not just by the local children (Saturday evening's free entertainment) but also by the local policeman (to make sure that the men were well out of the way when the train pulled out).

There was another, albeit unlikely, outlet for the men to have a wee dram – courtesy of the friendly society and temperance league, The Independent Order of Rechabites. (After the passing of the National Health Insurance Act in 1911, all workers had to belong to one of the recognised 'friendly societies', such as the Rechabites, to qualify for the (very small) pay-out in times of accident or illness.) The Philpstoun and District I.O.R. Pipe Band was set up in 1920 and until its demise before the war, it was much in demand for many an event near and far. It practised in the old hall at the Dairy.

Although there were plenty of Rechabites in the village, this was not a necessary qualification for playing in the band. Somehow, no one seemed to notice that the Philpstoun band were the only merry men at Rechabite events. When they played in Grangemouth they had to walk over the bridge out of town before they could find a pub, but such things were not a problem when the band went to Manchester for the 1935 Rechabite centenary. They arrived at 5am in unusually (for Manchester) pleasant weather to a city with all of its alcohol advertising covered up, dutifully played their best and then celebrated in a way that their patrons would definitely not have condoned.

The uniforms and instruments for the band were provided by the Rechabites, funded by dances and whist drives. In the 1930s the musicians were paid a fee of 12/6d each for the day. Johnny Sweeney, a championship-winning tenor drummer, explained that this paid your tea, paid your Mum your day off work and paid your girl into the shows. Johnny had learnt his art by cycling up to Polmont for a course and every Wednesday he would keep up with the new tricks by going into Edinburgh to watch the pipe band playing in the Princes Street gardens, then come home and practise the drummers' twirls day and night.

One of the most proficient players was the miner-come-chimney sweep Will Davidson, his skill known to all as he would frequently pipe himself home into the village from the bus stop at Gateside after being successful in competition (or just because it was a Saturday night and he felt like it) where The Rows

Philpstoun Pipe Band
Johnny Sweeney – tenor drummer – third from left front row.
(photograph courtesy of E Sweeney)

folk would be gathered outside to listen. During and after the days of the Philpstoun band, the men would often play with other local bands – a chance to play was rarely turned down.

There were other musical talents in the village, like Joe Savage who would play his fiddle down the back of The Rows so the young ones could dance. Johnny Docherty's family had a fiddle band with the Neilsons between the wars, Mick Cosgrove was also a dab hand on the violin and in the 1920s Philpstoun District even had its very own orchestra practising at the old bakery up the Dairy.

Then there was the fighting club and the homing – or 'doo' – club that had been around since at least 1910 and had pigeon lofts by the drying greens. (Proving the lasting popularity of doos, in November 1952 the Calderlin Property Company agreed to grant George Russell the lease of the garden at Number 1 House at the Old Farm for 10/- p.a. so that he could build a pigeon loft. He did have to put it in writing that he would correctly look after both the buildings and the pigeons, however).

The angling club would not only try their luck in the canal or the burn but would take off to Peebles or the Tweed on the bus on Friday night, coming home the next morning. They would light fires on the beach and fish all night – keeping warm with the occasional dram, of course. Their successes are not recorded, although the story of 'Pug' Sutherland (so-called because he drove one of the pugs up the lines to Bridgend) trying to hook a fishmonger's fish-shaped sign in Peebles hasn't been forgotten. As any fisherman knows, when the water is right it is hard to say no – Jock Sutherland was probably not the only one to turn back on the odd day on his way to work to get his rod when the burn was the right colour.

Another less physical pursuit was established by some of the local middle management in 1919 and would last until at least 1928: the Bridgend and District Mutual Improvement Association. Under the secretary – and treasurer-ship of Philpstoun's under-manager James Burns, they met in Bridgend School to discuss subjects such as 'which should be supreme: the Bible, the Church or conscience?', 'can a man get rich honestly?', 'should Parliament restrain excessive luxury?' and 'is happiness a delusion of youth and childhood?'.

Education may have been in short supply, but intelligence most surely was not. Take these quotes from the record books of the Association as evidence: 'the greatest spiritual tragedy of working class life is disclosed in the phrase that I never had a chance. Henceforth everyone should start with a nobleman's chance'. 'Education in the interests of society means making the man a better mechanic instead of making the mechanic a better man'. Discuss...

Bridgend School was also the original venue for meetings of the Brethren of Lodge Hopetoun St John (Freemasons), established in 1920 with members from Threemiletown, Bridgend, Linlithgow and of course Philpstoun.

By the 1950s, the event of the year was the Scottish Oils dance in the Assembly Rooms at Edinburgh. Everyone who worked for the company could go (assuming that they could afford the ticket and the full evening dress) so the day before it seemed as if the whole village decamped to Broxburn, with the ladies in the hairdressers and the men collecting their suits.

There were also a number of village outings. As well as the Sunday School trips, from the 1930s until well into the 1950s, the store used to run an annual train trip to Burntisland, the carriages gaily festooned with paper streamers.

Another memorable trip was to the Cowal Games in Dunoon, where some of the local children were participating in the dancing. A carriage had been booked on the train that was due to leave Philpstoun at 6.30 in the morning and Andrew Green dozed upright in his chair all night to be sure that they wouldn't miss it. After rising in good time to chap all the doors of those who were going, Andrew went home – where he promptly fell asleep...

Our Family (plus an old friend) c. 1936
Back row: Rose Savage, Denis McCrystal, Pat Savage, James Savage, (authors' father/grandfather, football referee), Joe Savage (violinist, lyricist etc.), Kate Savage
Front row: Mick Savage (football!) and his wife Annie
(photograph B Pattullo)

CHAPTER NINE

Shopping

WHEN ROSS BEGAN TO build the village, Crichton decreed that there would be only one shop, selling everything from fuel to food. The blacksmith, Post Office and sweetie shop at Old Philpstoun survived, as this agricultural community came under Hopetoun and had nothing to do with the works. The piggery at Champanys (one of the buildings that have now found a rather more upmarket role as a well-known restaurant) also continued to sell eggs.

There was also a post office at Burnside, where the villagers would keep any savings, especially if they were hoping to be married. The post itself was delivered daily – originally, of course, on foot and then later the postman was provided with a bicycle, then a motorcycle and eventually a small van. (Philpstoun did not get its own sub-post office until 27 January 1958 when Joe and Isa Millar, who managed the store, became the village's first sub-post master and post mistress, a job they would hold until 15 February 1985.)

Although there may have been only one actual shop in the early village, numerous travelling salesmen came from outside and plied their trade from horses' carts. Tailors, dressmakers, sellers of shoes and drapery, vendors of pots and pans and paraffin would all visit frequently, taking orders for later delivery or selling on the spot. Many of these were from the local Co-operative Stores at Bo'ness, Broxburn and West Calder. Payment was always on delivery – there was no credit.

In the early days of the village, one of the best remembered travelling salesmen came with a caravan-like shop selling almost everything, in the words of James Burns, 'from a needle to an anchor'. He liked to play the showman, running competitions among his audience (voting by show of hands often helping to ensure that the winner was a Philpstouner) and giving prizes to the winners. Once the crowd were sufficiently fired up, out would come the raffle book to sell tickets for the best 'prizes' – frequently clocks, many of which found their way into Philpstoun homes. On one memorable occasion Mr Burns' father-in-law, Mr Brown, even won a cockatoo which he apparently kept for 35 years, only giving it to the zoo when he couldn't get the right feed during the Second World War.

There were also grocery, butchers' and bakers' carts and from 1932, the

Mansons would bring their milk in from the Holdings on a cart pulled first by Ramsay, then Dixie, the horse with Maggie Manson at the reins (later to become Mrs Hugh Boyle, no great surprise to anyone who would watch Maggie pop in to say good morning to the Boyles most days). Dixie was liked, and fed, by the villagers: indeed if he was not given his customary piece by Mary Savage (despite the fact that the Savages took their milk from the Broxburn Co-op), he used to paw the ground – evidenced by the broken pavement outside number 32 Hope Street.

Private enterprise always finds its niche. In the 1920s and 30s, Mrs Kirkwood, a widow, supplemented her income by running an illicit shop in The Rows. She was famed among the children for selling sweeties from her scullery, unbeknownst, of course, to Mr Crichton.

Philpstoun's first shop was housed in Store Buildings, on the corner next to the Manse, opposite the hall. After David Gilchrist, the original storekeeper, left, the village was without a shop and totally dependent on the carts. Watching the Co-ops come in – the Broxburn Co-operative Society had even proposed that they open a branch in Philpstoun in 1915 – planted an idea in the heads of a number of local men, including Coby Watson's father and 'Captain' Henderson (so known for years after he had ceased to fill that role for Castlepark Thistle).

The Co-operative movement had started in 1812 with the Lennoxtown Friendly Victualling Society in Stirlingshire, closely followed by the Rochdale Pioneers. The obvious benefit was the dividend paid out to members based on the amount spent at the Co-op, providing both local loyalty and the incentive to make purchases. By the 1920s there were many regional Co-ops in Scotland – West Calder Co-op was established as early as 1875 – all independent but part of the Scottish Co-operative Society. Anything that could not be bought from an individual Co-op could be acquired via the main wholesalers.

The Philpstoun men formed a committee (President James Henderson; Vice President James Dickson; Secretary and Treasurer J Crombie junior; Board of Directors – Messrs D Dow, J Neilson, A Docherty, JF Burns, G Harvey, G McCulloch, W Watson and J Cunningham) and wrote to St Cuthbert's Co-operative Store in Edinburgh, the headquarters of the Scottish Co-operative Society, asking the directors to come out and give them advice. This they did and in 1922, the committee proceeded to set up Philpstoun's very own Co-op.

The Philpstoun & District Co-operative Society was inaugurated in June 1922 and was originally based in a large army hut on the site of the present store. The committee advertised for a manager and Mr Anderson from the Borders was the first to take the position. Although not all of the villagers turned away from the other Co-ops, the Philpstoun venture was so successful that in the first quarter they paid a 2/6d dividend.

On 17 March 1924, Ross agreed to let the shop and house at Store Buildings that had been the home of the Gilchrists to the Philpstoun & District Co-operative Society for £45/7/9d per annum, terms that the Society accepted on 22 March 1924.

Everyone was with one of the Co-ops. Saturday mornings would bring the 'cheque men' from the outside stores, who would sell the tokens – cheques – used for Co-op purchases. (For Philpstoun, the villagers just bought them over the counter.) Every cheque spent led to a dividend – hence while customers could pay by cash, it was not worthwhile to do so. There was also a 'mutuality club', into which members could pay a certain amount every week for 20 weeks and buy goods to its full value as soon as they had paid 3 instalments. That club book would usually be taken to one of the larger stores and used as proof of the member's right to purchase bigger items – perhaps shoes or hardware.

The Co-op man would come on Mondays to take the orders and someone else came back on Fridays to deliver the goods, and the bill. Literally everything could be bought at the Co-op with a 'line' – even furniture, which was collected from the wholesalers on Edinburgh's George Street or from Glasgow. Clothes were held in a shop in Pumpherston to which the store ran a special bus on dividend days.

The Philpstoun & District Co-operative Society went from strength to strength, even taking a lease from Ross for one of the old farm buildings up the Dairy (next to the old hall) for use as a bakery. The let ran from 1 December 1924 (rent set at £24 per annum) until Whit Sunday 1932. The baker and his barrow of bread became a common sight in the village.

However following the closure of the Philpstoun works, some of the villagers became nervous about their money and pulled it out of the Co-op. Worried that the rest might lose their money, the committee decided to sell out to West Calder in 1932 before this could happen. The official let of the shop by Ross to the West Calder Co-operative Society was dated 2 April 1932 and the shopkeeper, William Bell, took over the house at 11 Store Buildings. (He would later be replaced as manager by Pete West from Winchburgh.) West Calder built the stone building next to the Church as well as the bungalow for the manager that still stand today.

Only during the Second World War did the Co-op carts not come to Philpstoun (although the Mansons and their milk still made the rounds), and that was simply because they were not allowed in – Philpstoun was a restricted zone. Some Broxburn customers stayed loyal though, going up to the Red Rows at Threemiletown where the grocery van stopped (where the locals very kindly let the Philpstoun women go to the head of the queue so they could catch the return bus) or over to Old Philpstoun for the butcher's van on Saturday mornings. After the war the Co-ops quickly came back, this time in vans thanks to the availability of petrol – for example Broxburn Co-op's hardware van came in on a Thursday and the drapery van on a Monday.

While everything could be bought via the store, other tradesmen did, of course, survive, like the popular outfitters Hardy of Bathgate and Coulters of Broxburn with their ironmongers' van, and of course the shops in Linlithgow. Most of these merchants also allowed their customers to pay by the week, letting them put down enough to buy a suit or a new bicycle perhaps.

There was also Johnny Docherty: miner by day, hairdresser to both men and women by night (the same one with the fiddle band – a man of many talents). His building – well, a green wooden shed to be accurate – behind the Manse on the Dairy was countenanced as he was not a shop, but providing a service.

In the 1930s and 40s, Tommy Reape from Linlithgow would come out to the village selling fish and chips from his cart, pulled by Charlie the horse: so confident was Charlie of the route that he would trot along unsupervised quite happily while his master cooked his wares over the coal fire on the cart. The chips would be served out in newspaper – Tommy Hamilton remembers that his mother would collect old papers for Mr Reape and that if the bairns collected up a big bag of grass for Charlie, they would get a free poke of chips in return.

Mr Reape kept up his rounds during the war, even selling to the soldiers at the army camp down Pardovan Road. After the war Bill Duncan from Linlithgow gradually took over and would come out to the village two or three evenings a week, well into the 1950s, with his chip van. The fish and chips were cooked in the van, again on coal fires, and people queued up to be served from an opening in the side of the van. Later he purchased an old bus that had slightly more style – people could queue *inside* the bus.

The Cabrellis came around with ice cream too in the 1940s and 1950s, not with a van but a black Morris 10 car. The ice cream was kept in a double skinned canister (rather like a thermos flask), with ice between the sides to keep it cold, that stood in the back of the car while customers were served through the front window. Later they did invest in a van, as did Duncans of Winchburgh – the brothers of the above-cited chip man.

Mick Cosgrove was already working in a shop in Linlithgow and had been asked to establish a Sub-Post Office in Philpstoun by the Postmaster General. He had originally hoped to build something close to Pardovan, but Mr Crichton refused him permission. Instead Mick started to sell newspapers and periodicals from home, the Linlithgow man Danny Logue having by now stopped delivering them to the village with his horse and cart. During the Second World War Mick left for the army but others kept his business alive for him, not least his sisters. (Mick's blue Austin, bought in 1938, was one of the first cars in the village but had to be replaced after the war, having spent six years rusting in an unheated garage).

After he came home Mr Keddie gave him permission to take over Johnny Docherty's hut, the latter having left for Winchburgh. Helped by his sister Hannah, Mick sold groceries, sweets, cigarettes, stationery, stockings and the like between one and eight o'clock. He also had newspapers, collected from the station in the morning (until it closed) and from Gateside in the evening, which were delivered by a succession of village lads (like Andrew Burns), as well as Christmas annuals. He or his sister Mary would come around on a Friday evening to collect the money for the deliveries.

Mick also carried odd bits and pieces like confetti, to the relief of visiting wedding guests, if not necessarily to the bride!

CHAPTER TEN

The Second World War

MINING BEING A PROTECTED profession, most Philpstoun men were not allowed to enlist when the Second World War broke out. Following Anthony Eden's May 1940 broadcast calling for local defence volunteers, every last one of them thus tried to sign up for the Home Guard (affiliated to the Royal Scots), led by Platoon Commander Andrew Moffat, formerly of the Scots Guards. This created problems of its own as there were just too many for them all to be accepted, so some went to the fire service in Linlithgow, cycling in after work, and others joined the ARP – everyone helped somehow.

The best vantage point for watching The Forth was the tower at The Binns. The Binns (named for the Gaelic for hills, 'beins') had been the home of the Dalyell family since 1612 (and still is). Everyone in the area knew of its most famous resident and the founder of the Royal Scots Greys in 1681, General Tam, otherwise known as 'Bluidy Tam' for his treatment of Covenanters. Legend has it if he was not rolling his prisoners down hills in spiked barrels, he was roasting them alive in the Binns' bakehouse. Logic apparently put paid to the latter idea as there was not an oven big enough to roast a Covenanter at the house, or so they thought... until just such an oven was discovered behind a false wall in the bakehouse in 1937.

General Tam was also believed to associate with the devil himself. In about 1640 a beautiful table of marble inlaid with semi-precious stones was brought to the house, only to disappear without trace some 40 years later. Local lore had it that it was at this very table that the General and the devil played their nightly card games. Every night the devil won – except one, when Tam cheated. So outraged was the devil that he threw the table at Tam, who ducked and the table landed in the pond, not be seen again until the drought of 1879.

Clean that table as you might, one corner still bears the shape of the devil's hoof. Some people may claim that the table was simply stolen, was far too heavy to carry so the thieves prised out the stones and dumped the table in the pond, and others still say it was hidden there on purpose, but the authors reserve the privilege to prefer the first story. Either way, General Tam and his horse have been said to ride the house and estate ever since.

On a still night, you can hear the cries of the Binns' peacocks down in

Philpstoun. Add the fear of the war and it is perhaps not too surprising that some of the younger Guards were – reportedly – nervous about being alone in the tower at night, but Bob Crichton well remembers being at the top of the tower during an air raid. There was another lookout tower at the bing. The Binns tower was also considered as a site for anti-aircraft guns to guard the Forth Bridge and shipping, but it was deemed too far from the targets.

The war did not disrupt the mines, with the men setting off to work on their bicycles, dodging shrapnel if the occasion arose. (Indeed, the threat of hostilities had prompted increased investment in the industry and with Grangemouth closed during the war, there was less competitive pressure.) A new use was found for the old Philpstoun works, which the men cleaned and whitewashed and set up as an air-raid shelter, complete with seating and a stove. There were also regular night shifts, both in the mine and at the bings.

Evidence of the size of the mines is in the 1945 Government tables, which say that Duddingston nos. 3 and 4, no. 1 Totleywells (Duddingston) and Philpstoun 1 and 6 (Whitequarries) were employing respectively 114, 91, 146 and 81 below ground, with 28, 21, 36 and 24 above. (According to the table, all of these mines were, by this time, the property of the Oakbank Oil Company with Robert Keddie as area manager.)

The farms did suffer, as the exemption for farmers' families only allowed the owner and one man of service age to stay at the farm, while the others went to war, the mines or Nobels. (Nobels Explosives Factory was set up in Linlithgow in 1901, and during both wars it made munitions, providing employment for many of the village girls and some of the men. Later it began to produce pharmaceuticals, eventually to be bought by ICI.) In their place came landgirls and at the end of the war, prisoners of war from the camp at Abercorn.

During the war years, everything was carefully rationed. It was a time for necessities, not luxuries: even toilet paper was quickly replaced by cut-up newspapers. Farmers certainly could not choose what to do with their produce. The daily egg collection was sent to a packing station and in return, the farmer received enough feed for the producing number of hens. A farmer with less than 25 hens did not have to send his eggs away but he was also not given any feed. The result was that no one kept back their eggs – there was no point when you could not feed the birds.

The same system applied to milk: 20 milkers' worth gave you feed coupons to buy the protein that 20 milk cows required. As Tommy Hamilton described it, it was as if 'the coos had ration books too'. As for produce, the miller would count your bags, send the tally to the inspectors and they would tell you how much the Government wanted. Inspectors would also do the rounds after harvest and estimate how much any given area should have yielded. The perfect bureaucratic foils to any potential black market. Anyone found with unaccounted-for produce was in for short shrift: the Holdings did not even dare to give milk away in case they were reported.

Everyone contributed something to the war effort. Door to door collections were carried out by Mrs Hardie and Mr Paterson to ensure that the village had additional first aid materials in case of need and raffles and concerts were held for the Red Cross.

The Philpstoun men may not have gone to war, but the war very definitely came to Philpstoun. At about 3 o'clock in the afternoon of 16 October 1939, Elizabeth Sweeney was preparing her husband's dinner as he was shortly due back from his shift at Duddingston (in fact, she had just put the potatoes on) when the first shrapnel fell, the result of the Luftwaffe's somewhat off-target attempt to bomb ships moored down river from the Forth Bridge in Scotland's first air raid. (There was a troop train on the Bridge at the time as well, but they missed that too.) The men who were cycling home at the time saw the planes right enough, but thinking they were ours, they waved – at first.

No one knew what was happening and no one had seen shrapnel before, but there was definitely something falling all over Hope Street. Listening to the news that night, the Sweeneys, like many of their friends, were bemused to hear Lord

John and Elizabeth Sweeney
(photograph courtesy of E Sweeney)

Haw Haw broadcasting that 'the peasants had been out in the fields cheering the brave pilots'. Mrs Sweeney was, in fact, watching from the scullery window. Listeners of Lord Haw Haw please take note. It was only the next morning when the papers arrived that the villagers found out what had actually happened.

Given its proximity to the Forth, Philpstoun suffered its fair share of air raids, waking the residents with the siren, anti-aircraft guns and search lights and sending them hurrying for the shelters. As well as the shelter at the mine, there were stone shelters built behind The Rows – but they were simple brick structures with flat roofs, with no particular support. (Perhaps that explained why my grandmother, while my grandfather worked nights in the mine, calmly announced that if she and my (then baby) mother were to die, it would be in their own home, thank you, and never went near a shelter. Perhaps she was just being my Granny.)

Three bombs fell in a nearby field in 1939, the result of a dogfight between a British fighter and German bomber, but while some of the windows on Hope Street were blown in, luckily no one was killed.

James Burns was appointed as the chief air raid warden and he was responsible, as well as his administrative tasks, for patrolling the Avenue Houses together with William Mitchell. Messrs West, Clelland and Paris were the wardens for Castlepark, Station Road and the station; James Kent and John Geekie took Pardovan cottages and smallholdings; Hope Street was under Donald Ramsay, Andrew Moffat, Joe Savage and Pat Savage; while James Paterson and A Gilmour had Rosoline Place, the Manse, Store Buildings and Kinnaird Terrace. According to the papers that Mr Burns submitted to the Linlithgow ARP HQ, the Philpstoun district stretched from Duncan's smallholding at Sunnyside to the North, Walker's farm at Fairniehill to the South, the station to the East and Mr Thomson's smallholding at West Park to the West.

Everyone was issued with a gas mask at the hall by James Burns and his team to keep with them at all times along with their identity cards – a total of 550 masks were taken from the Linlithgow depot for the Philpstoun district. Any child arriving at school without either was sent straight home to fetch them. Unlike most schools, St Joseph's Catholic Primary did not have its own bomb shelters as it was decided that the children would be far safer in the dungeons of Linlithgow Palace; air raid drills were a regular feature of school life as from October 1939.

Adults too knew to carry their papers at all times. Mr Clelland could confirm that. Every morning he would go to meet his wife from the bus at Gateside as she was working nights as a nurse. One day he was stopped by the Philpstoun policeman and George McCulloch, who was a special constable during the war, and asked for his identity papers. It didn't matter that they knew full well who he was – he didn't have them and he was in a whole lot of trouble. As for walking out on the country roads after black-out, you may as well have hung a sign around your neck asking to be stopped by the police, for you just about always were.

The gas masks came in small, medium and large sizes. Children were of course none too keen on wearing them, so their masks were shaped like Mickey Mouse. They would be regularly checked both by Mr Burns and, less meticulously, by teachers at the schools. There were also large folding contraptions in which babies under two were supposed to sit.

Thanks to Mr Burns maintaining a list of the gas masks issued in 1939, we have a record of Philpstoun's residents at that time, by address, surname and number of masks:

Castlepark
Crichton, 3
Allan, 2 (the maids)

No	Hope Street	No	
1	Kerr, 3	19	Paterson, 4
2		20	Malloy, 6
3	Leadbetter, 4	21	McKelvie, 2
4	Clark, 4	22	Lowe, 1
5	Newton, 3	23	Clark, 2
6	Stein, 4	24	McArdle, 3
7	Ford, 3	25	Sutherland, 4
8	Malcolmson, 5	26	Meikle, 3
9			Davidson, 1
10	McKeon, 3	27	Wilkinson, 3
	McKenna, 1	28	Sutherland, 3
11	Allan, 2		Davies, 1
12	Byrne, 6	29	McMahon, 3
	Harkins, 1	30	McCrystal, 2
13	Cosgrove, 5	31	McKenzie, 2
14	Reid, 5		Fleming, 1
15	Savage, 3	32	Savage, 2
	Mullan, 3	33	Gartland, 2
16	Sweeney, 2	34	Kirkwood, 2
17	Robertson, 2	35	Flood, 7
18	Walker, 2	36	Moffat, 4

No	Name	No	Name
37	Boyle, 8	62	Paterson, 1
38	Caulfield, 7	63	Bryce, 2
39	Meikle, 6	64	Provan, 2
40		65	Brown, 2
41	Green, 4	66	Cowan, 6
42	Johnstone, 2	67	Brown, 3
43	McArdle, 7	68	Paterson, 2
44	O'Donnell, 8	69	Noble, 3
45	Kerr, 4		Newton, 1
46	Ward, 5	70	McCulloch, 6
47		71	Kerr, 5
48	Sweeney, 2	72	Ford, 4
49	Ramsay, 4	73	Morrison, 2
50	McKnight, 5	74	Munro, 2
51	Davidson, 4	75	Stein, 7
52	Kilbride, 4	76	McCulloch, 3
53	Ward, 6	77	McEwan, 3
54	Davis, 1	78	Hardie, 4
55	Burns, 6	79	Russell, 1
56	Muir, 4	80	Docherty, 4
57	Kilpatrick, 1	81	Gault, 3
	Kelp, 1	82	Russell, 2
58	Kerr, 3	83	Ford, 3
59	Breadon, 4	84	Stirton, 2
60	Currie, 4	??	Stewart, 2
61	Stein, 3		

No	The Dairy	No	
	Carr, 1		Russell, 3
	Houston, 1		Stewart, 1

No	The Avenue	No	
1	Burns, 6		Forbes, 4
11	Henderson, 5		Thomson, 1
	Neilson, 5		Stein, 7
	Anderson, 5		Wilson, 2
	Stirton, 3		Allan, 2
	Hogg, 3		Docherty, 3
	Swan, 6		

No	Rosoline Place	No	
2	Dow, 3		Johnstone, 4
2	Crawford, 1		Pryde, 7
3	Crombie, 2		

No	Kinnaird Terrace	No	
1	Lyon, 3	4	Scott, 5
2	Grant, 7	4	Mushet, 1
3	Orr, 9	4	Dickson, 1

No	Store Buildings	No	
2	Allan, 2		Paterson, 3
5	Kilpatrick, 2		Campbell, 3
9	Muir, 4		McLaughlan, 2
10	Gilmour, 3		Mitchell, 1
11	Stein, 4		Stevins, 1
11	Alan, 1		Johnstone, 1
12	Gault, 2		Moyes, 2

No	Station Cottages	No	
	Wallace, 2		Fleming, 2
	Mitchell, 6		Cosgrove, 7

Station House	The Manse
Forrest, 2	Philip, 2
	Hardie, 1

No	Pardovan	No	
4	Bathgate, 2		Crockett, 1
7	Hamilton, 3		Kent, 5
8	Fulton, 3		Millar, 3
8	Nicolson, 3		Paris, 4
9	Blackley, 1		Davis, 1
	Scott, 2		Adams, 1
	Geekie, 3		McFarland, 3
	West, 5		Lawrie, 2

Sunnylea Pardovan	Sunnyside Pardovan
Addison, 3	Duncan, 5
	Blackley, 1

Pardovan Bridge	Hough Farm
Adam, 4	Manson, 10

Westfield	West End
Paterson, 5	Clelland, 3

West Park	The Cottage
Thomson, 3	McIlraith, 2

Fairniehill
Walker, 3

Philpstoun was cut off from the outside world for the duration of the war as a restricted zone, due to the major army camps at Merrylees at the bottom of Pardovan Road, before the Queensferry Road, and at Totleywells. (The guns at these camps were retained until well after the war had finished). The residents were allowed out, with a pass, but outsiders could not get in – Mrs Sweeney's mother even needed permission from the police to come to escort her daughter's new baby to the christening.

All available land was cultivated during the war, including the football pitch that Mr Addison had as a cornfield as he had lost some of his land to the army camp. The goalposts and the rails around the field were taken away for scrap and the team was disbanded, although some of the lads would go down to Blackness for a kick about, as its field was not suitable for agricultural use. The old hall, meanwhile, found yet another use in its multi-purpose history and became the meeting place for the Home Guard.

The war at least brought one new idea to Philpstoun. It was the influx of English soldiers and Polish prisoners of war, many of the latter helping in the tattie gathering and going on to settle permanently in the area, that started the tradition of Christmas trees and the true celebration of the event.

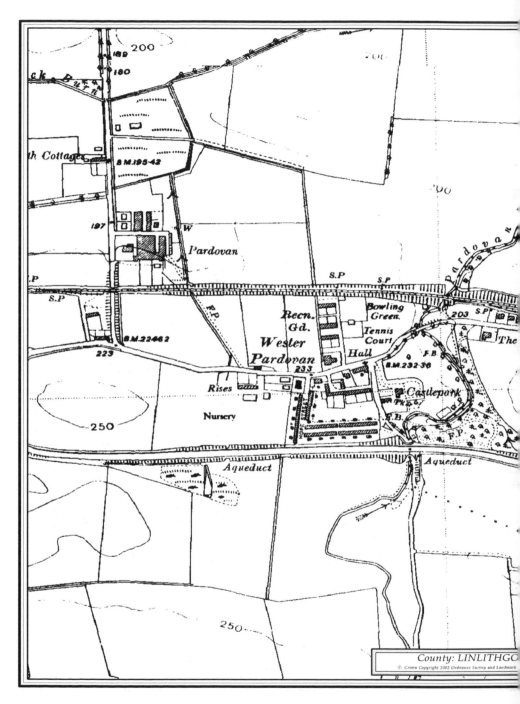

1952 Map

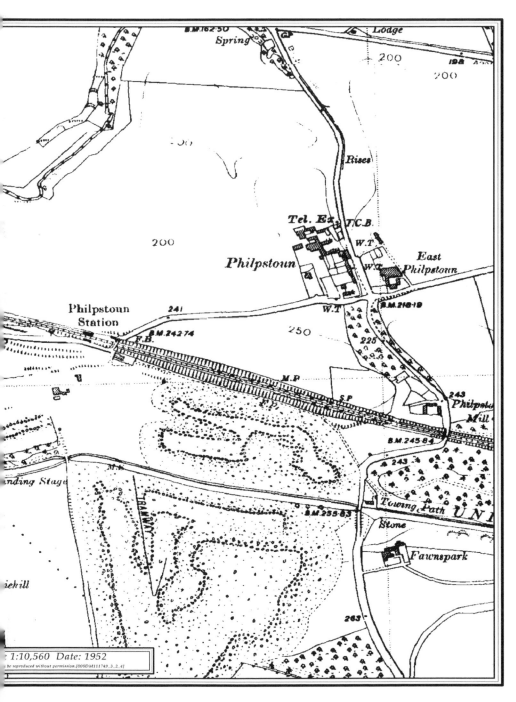

(Crown Copyright and Landmark Information Group Ltd, all rights reserved 2004)

CHAPTER ELEVEN

The End

SHALE MINING IS A BUSINESS and, by the 1950s, it was not a very profitable one. Imports of far cheaper crude oil resumed in 1945 and the death knell for the Scottish shale industry was tolling.

The mines were closed gradually but steadily from the 1950s. On 3 April 1962, R Gilchrist of the Oakbank Oil Company wrote to the Hopetoun Estate Development Company to say 'I very much regret to inform you that the Board of Directors have decided, with great reluctance, to discontinue the mining and retorting of oil shale within the next few weeks'. Citing the Government's decision to eliminate the duty preference (as a result of the UK joining EFTA) he said that this decision 'renders the cessation of oil shale mining and retorting inevitable. The Company has therefore decided that it would be in the best interests of the employees to cease operations in the immediate future while other industrial projects now being established in the district provide favourable prospects of alternative employment'.

Mr Gilchrist went on to say that 'arrangements are being made to cease the mining operations at Nos. 1 and 6 Mines Philpstoun on or about 4th May, after which date only a few men will be retained for the withdrawal of plant etc.'

Formal notice followed terminating the mineral lease. On 5 April the Hopetoun factor, JN Douglas Menzies, replied that 'it is indeed going to be a great blow to the district as a whole when your operations cease and I note with much regret that this is going to be very soon now. We all hope here that the vast majority of your many workpeople will have no difficulty in obtaining alternative employment as soon as possible'.

The last mine closed in May 1962 and all but the men at Pumpherston refinery and Grangemouth were dismissed.

Although the workers knew that closure was on the cards, in the event they were given only two or three weeks' actual notice, with a skeleton staff kept on at each site to effect the closing. The men who had been with the company for 25 years got the standard long-service bonus – a choice of three gifts, each costing £50: a Longines watch, a tea set or a clock. The others got nothing. Those that were under 65 at the time never received a pension.

Philpstoun was no longer to be run by Scottish Oils. West Lothian Council

Closure of the mine 1962
(photograph courtesy of The Almond Valley Heritage Centre)

had already moved in and built Pardovan Crescent, on which work had started in the 1930s but had been stopped by the war. The scheme was eventually finished in 1952, when it became the new home of many former Rows' residents, and other local families, allocated on a points system (number in family etc.) for houses with two or three bedrooms. (The rents were of course slightly higher, and there was certainly more room, but they weren't quite the same. Impressive a lady as old Mrs Cosgrove may have been, and as nice as her new house might be, she would freely admit that she missed her seat on the old bucket.)

The Rows had already started to be demolished, and would soon be replaced by Church Court, completed in 1968. This at least was the work of a local man. Past Pardovan House on the right used to be a pig farm, and on the left two cottages, homes to the Connors and the Harrisons. Of the latter, the eldest son lost an arm at Arnhem and the other became a joiner, eventually opening his own building firm, which became very successful. It was to him that the Council turned to build Church Court after the demolition of the Rows which, being a local, he wanted to make his showpiece.

Scottish Oils offered the residents of The Avenue the chance to buy their houses at the standard price of £100 per apartment, hence £200 or £300 a house depending on the number of rooms, all fees included. The residents were given a couple of weeks to think about the offer: not many needed to take that long. No such deal was offered to other residents – but then The Rows were not really saleable.

Mr Crichton died at Castlepark in 1966 and this house too passed into private hands.

The new houses were built and gradually people moved in, or moved away. The men scattered to jobs in the new Leyland plant at Bathgate, or the younger ones to BP in Grangemouth – to whatever they could find. 79 years after The Philpstoun Oil Co. arrived, Scottish Oils finally left.

While no-one can claim that the Council has not looked after the village, the Philpstoun of this tale is long gone. It was hard, it was basic – but it was a true community, and a true home.

Remember that next time you take the train into Waverley. And the next time that your Granny starts to tell of the old days, catch her on tape, unless you want her stories to disappear forever.

Acknowledgements

WHY WOULD TWO WOMEN, respectively living in London and Brussels, research and write a book about a wee village in Scotland? We hope that, having read it, you will understand why – because we felt that we had to.

My mother, Barbara Pattullo, was born into Philpstoun just before the Second World War, the only child of miner James Savage and his wife Mary. My grandfather died in 1954 and my mother left the village to work in London in 1956 but my grandmother lived there almost until the day she died in 1982.

James Savage
(photograph B Pattullo)

As children, my brothers and I spent many holidays at 23 Church Court, playing in the gardens and the park, walking our dog along the canal and listening to Granny's friends and neighbours talk of how it used to be. This is their story, not mine.

Dates and major events are a matter of public record: personal memories are not. We are indebted to the residents of Philpstoun, past and present, who were prepared to dwell on days gone by and answer any number of impertinent questions. We know that we have only managed to scratch the surface of the real history of Philpstoun's mining days, so we beg indulgence for any omissions or oversights – none are deliberate. We have also done our level best to ensure that everything is correct – my apologies for any mistakes that have made it into this final version, responsibility for which is mine alone.

Mary Savage
(photograph B Pattullo)

Especial thanks are due to Mr and Mrs Martin Philbin, not least for helping to organise many of the original interviews that formed the basis of this work, to Miss Betty Burns for allowing us to see her father's papers and to Mrs Linda Hamilton for sharing with us her papers on local history. Mr and Mrs William (Coby) Watson, Mr and Mrs Johnny Sweeney, Mr and Mrs Peter Mushet and Mr and Mrs Robert

(Bob) Crichton gave us their time, their hospitality and many a story of folk, mines and sport and Mr and Mrs Tommy Hamilton helped us townies to understand something about farming. Our thanks to all of them for the loan of, and the permission to reproduce, their personal photographs. We have tried to ensure that the right names are with the right faces: again, apologies for any errors which are most unintentional.

Without BP, this book would not have appeared. Our gratitude especially to Ian Howarth, Ian Smith and Jim Doherty for understanding what we were trying to do, and why, as well as to the archivists of BP at the University of Warwick, and, of course, to the irreplaceable Robin Hadfield. Tam Dalyell MP did us the honour of providing a preface, John H McKay, former Lord Provost of Edinburgh and renowned shale expert, very kindly gave us invaluable comments and our thanks also go to Pat the Cope Gallagher, Irish Minister of State at the Department of Environment and Local Government, for stepping in when the bookshops failed us and providing a copy of his grandfather's book *My Story*.

Votes of thanks also to Gavin MacDougall at Luath Press, to miscellaneous fact providers and general historians Alan Cook and Adam Bruce and to George Farmer, Alexander Benczek and John Chave for support and proof-reading. Personal thanks also to MPH Christophe Zimmermann, for trying to understand: JTTF.

The biggest vote of thanks, however, is reserved for the late Misses Mary and Hannah Cosgrove. It was Miss Mary Cosgrove's tales of Philpstoun life that were the original inspiration for this work, prompting the comment 'it makes you want to record her' leading to the now infamous response from Ken Pattullo – husband, father and editor-in-chief – 'well, why don't you?'.

Thanks Dad.

Marie Pattullo
Brussels, 2004

SOCIAL HISTORY

Shale Voices

Alistair Findlay
foreword by Tam Dalyell MP
ISBN 0 946487 63 4 PBK £10.99
ISBN 0 946487 78 2 HBK £17.99

'He was at Addiewell oil works. Anyone goes in there is there for keeps.' JOE, Electrician

'There's shale from here to Ayr, you see.' DICK, a Drawer

'The way I describe it is, you're a coal miner and I'm a shale miner. You're a tramp and I'm a toff.' HARRY, a Drawer

'There were sixteen or eighteen Simpsons... ...She was having one every dividend we would say.' SISTERS, from Broxburn

Shale Voices offers a fascinating insight into shale mining, an industry that employed generations of Scots, had an impact on the social, political and cultural history of Scotland and gave birth to today's large oil companies. Author Alistair Findlay was born in the shale mining village of Winchburgh and is the fourth son of a shale miner, Bob Findlay, who became editor of the *West Lothian Courier*. *Shale Voices* combines oral history, local journalism and family history. The generations of communities involved in shale mining provide, in their own words, a unique documentation of the industry and its cultural and political impact.

Photographs, drawings, poetry and short stories make this a thought provoking and entertaining account. It is as much a joy to dip into and feast the eyes on as to read from cover to cover.

'Alistair Findlay has added a basic source material to the study of Scottish history that is invaluable and will be of great benefit to future generations. Scotland owes him a debt of gratitude for undertaking this work.'
TAM DALYELL MP

'...lovingly evoked ...isn't an idle intellectual exercise ...laid out in poetic form, captures the music of speech ...love & respect shines through in this book ...one of the finest pieces of social history I've ever read.'
MARK STEVEN, THE SCOTTISH CONNECTION, BBC RADIO SCOTLAND

'...for thousands of people across the country their attitudes, lifestyles and opinions have been formed through an industry which was once the envy of the world ...captures the essence of the feelings of the time.'
LINDSAY GOULD, WEST LOTHIAN COURIER

'...the mighty shale bings of West Lothian seem to be a secret which remarkably few outsiders share. how beautifully their russet grit glows in dawn or evening light.'
ANGUS CALDER, THE SCOTSMAN

'Findlay records their voices, as sharp and red as the rock they worked ...their voices are also, in a strange way, freed. Findlay, himself a poet, lays them out on the page as poetry to capture the "dynamics of conversation". The result is to recreate the directness, simplicity and power of everyday speech.'
JOHN FOSTER, THE MORNING STAR

'...the real and rounded history of the people ...important, informative, captivating and inspiring, speckled with hardship and humour, it is well worth a read.'
JOHN STEVENSON, SCOTLAND IN UNISON

'...the class solidarity and sense of sharing with neighbours in good times and bad could enhance the world of today. Alistair Findlay says it much better than I can... do you not feel echoes of Lewis Grassic Gibbon's Sunset Song in this man's writing?'
WILLIAM WOLFE, SCOTS INDEPENDENT

Pumpherston: the story of a shale oil village

Sybil Cavanagh, John H McKay, James O'Hagan and Kneale Johnson

ISBN 1 84282 011 7 HB £17.99

ISBN 1 84282 015 X PB £10.99

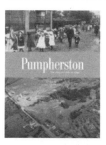

Pumpherston – surely one of the strangest place-names in Lowland Scotland – has a history that is as unusual as its name. The ancient castle and lands of Pumpherston evolved into a fertile estate with an experimental farm, and those in turn gave way to one of the world's most successful early oil companies. The Pumpherston story includes a huntsman eaten by his own hounds, a bankrupt MP and a golf course enlivened by cows – and cow-pats.

In 1884 the Pumpherston Oil Works was built and a substantial village came into being. The Pumpherston Oil Company is seen in the wider context of the shale oil industry. The story of its successes and failures is followed through the era of Scottish Oils and BP to the close-down of the shale oil industry in Scotland in 1962.

The village was built, supervised and patronised by the oil companies. A strange culture emerged in which the employers intervened in all aspects of their employees' lives, whether at work, at home or at leisure.

This fascinating book also looks at the rich social life that grew up in the village, and the wealth of characters – high achievers as well as eccentric worthies – that will stir the memories of everyone who grew up in or remembers Pumpherston in the old days.

And the story of Pumpherston comes full circle with the cleaning up of the oil works site. BP has used pioneering technology to clear the site of the pollution from more than a century of work, and to return the area to its original rural nature.

A rich mix of historical, technical and anecdotal material makes up a book that will appeal to readers not just in the local area, but to 'Pumphy' exiles all over the world and to anyone interested in the shale oil industry and Scotland's industrial heritage.

NATURAL WORLD

The Hydro Boys: pioneers of renewable energy
Emma Wood
ISBN 1 84282 047 8 PB £8.99

Wild Scotland
James McCarthy
photographs by Laurie Campbell
ISBN 0 946487 37 5 PB £8.99

Wild Lives: Otters – On the Swirl of the Tide
Bridget MacCaskill
ISBN 0 946487 67 7 PB £9.99

Wild Lives: Foxes – The Blood is Wild
Bridget MacCaskill
ISBN 0 946487 71 5 PB £9.99

Scotland – Land & People: An Inhabited Solitude
James McCarthy
ISBN 0 946487 57 X PB £7.99

The Highland Geology Trail
John L Roberts
ISBN 0 946487 36 7 PB £5.99

Red Sky at Night
John Barrington
ISBN 0 946487 60 X PB £8.99

Listen to the Trees
Don MacCaskill
ISBN 0 946487 65 0 PB £9.99

THE QUEST FOR

The Quest for the Celtic Key
Karen Ralls-MacLeod and
Ian Robertson
ISBN 0 946487 73 1 HB £18.99
ISBN 1 84282 031 1 PB £8.99

The Quest for Arthur
Stuart McHardy
ISBN 1 84282 012 5 HB £16.99

The Quest for the Nine Maidens
Stuart McHardy
ISBN 0 946487 66 9 HB £16.99

The Quest for Charles Rennie Mackintosh
John Cairney
ISBN 1 84282 058 3 HB £16.99

The Quest for Robert Louis Stevenson
John Cairney
ISBN 0 946487 87 1 HB £16.99

The Quest for the Original Horse Whisperers
Russell Lyon
ISBN 1 84282 020 6 HB £16.99

ON THE TRAIL OF

On the Trail of the Pilgrim Fathers
J. Keith Cheetham
ISBN 0 946487 83 9 PB £7.99

On the Trail of Mary Queen of Scots
J. Keith Cheetham
ISBN 0 946487 50 2 PB £7.99

On the Trail of John Wesley
J. Keith Cheetham
ISBN 1 84282 023 0 PB £7.99

On the Trail of William Wallace
David R. Ross
ISBN 0 946487 47 2 PB £7.99

On the Trail of Robert the Bruce
David R. Ross
ISBN 0 946487 52 9 PB £7.99

On the Trail of Robert Service
GW Lockhart
ISBN 0 946487 24 3 PB £7.99

On the Trail of John Muir
Cherry Good
ISBN 0 946487 62 6 PB £7.99

On the Trail of Robert Burns
John Cairney
ISBN 0 946487 51 0 PB £7.99

On the Trail of Bonnie Prince Charlie
David R Ross
ISBN 0 946487 68 5 PB £7.99

On the Trail of Queen Victoria in the Highlands
Ian R Mitchell
ISBN 0 946487 79 0 PB £7.99

ISLANDS

The Islands that Roofed the World: Easdale, Belnahua, Luing & Seil:
Mary Withall
ISBN 0 946487 76 6 PB £4.99

Rum: Nature's Island
Magnus Magnusson
ISBN 0 946487 32 4 PB £7.95

LUATH GUIDES TO SCOTLAND

The North West Highlands: Roads to the Isles
Tom Atkinson
ISBN 0 946487 54 5 PB £4.95

Mull and Iona: Highways and Byways
Peter Macnab
ISBN 0 946487 58 8 PB £4.95

The Northern Highlands: The Empty Lands
Tom Atkinson
ISBN 0 946487 55 3 PB £4.95

The West Highlands: The Lonely Lands
Tom Atkinson
ISBN 0 946487 56 1 PB £4.95

South West Scotland
Tom Atkinson
ISBN 0 946487 04 9 PB £4.95

TRAVEL & LEISURE

Die Kleine Schottlandfibel [Scotland Guide in German]
Hans-Walter Arends
ISBN 0 946487 89 8 PB £8.99

Let's Explore Berwick-upon-Tweed
Anne Bruce English
ISBN 1 84282 029 X PB £4.99

Let's Explore Edinburgh Old Town
Anne Bruce English
ISBN 0 946487 98 7 PB £4.99

Edinburgh's Historic Mile
Duncan Priddle
ISBN 0 946487 97 9 PB £2.99

Pilgrims in the Rough: St Andrews beyond the 19th hole
Michael Tobert
ISBN 0 946487 74 X PB £7.99

FOOD & DRINK

The Whisky Muse: Scotch whisky in poem & song
various, compiled and edited by Robin Laing
ISBN 1 84282 041 9 PB £7.99

First Foods Fast: how to prepare good simple meals for your baby
Lara Boyd
ISBN 1 84282 002 8 PB £4.99

Edinburgh and Leith Pub Guide
Stuart McHardy
ISBN 0 946487 80 4 PB £4.95

WALK WITH LUATH

Skye 360: walking the coastline of Skye
Andrew Dempster
ISBN 0 946487 85 5 PB £8.99

Walks in the Cairngorms
Ernest Cross
ISBN 0 946487 09 X PB £4.95

Short Walks in the Cairngorms
Ernest Cross
ISBN 0 946487 23 5 PB £4.95

The Joy of Hillwalking
Ralph Storer
ISBN 0 946487 28 6 PB £7.50

Scotland's Mountains before the Mountaineers
Ian R Mitchell
ISBN 0 946487 39 1 PB £9.99

Mountain Days & Bothy Nights
Dave Brown & Ian R Mitchell
ISBN 0 946487 15 4 PB £7.50

BIOGRAPHY

The Last Lighthouse
Sharma Krauskopf
ISBN 0 946487 96 0 PB £7.99

Tobermory Teuchter
Peter Macnab
ISBN 0 946487 41 3 PB £7.99

Bare Feet & Tackety Boots
Archie Cameron
ISBN 0 946487 17 0 PB £7.95

Come Dungeons Dark
John Taylor Caldwell
ISBN 0 946487 19 7 PB £6.95

SOCIAL HISTORY

A Word for Scotland
Jack Campbell
ISBN 0 946487 48 0 PB £12.99

Crofting Years
Francis Thompson
ISBN 0 946487 06 5 PB £6.95

HISTORY

Desire Lines: A Scottish Odyssey
David R Ross
ISBN 1 84282 033 8 PB £9.99

Civil Warrior: extraordinary life & poems of Montrose
Robin Bell
ISBN 1 84282 013 3 HB £10.99

FOLKLORE

Scotland: Myth, Legend & Folklore
Stuart McHardy
ISBN 0 946487 69 3 PB £7.99

Luath Storyteller: Highland Myths & Legends
George W Macpherson
ISBN 1 84282 003 6 PB £5.00

Tales of the North Coast
Alan Temperley
ISBN 0 946487 18 9 PB £8.99

Tall Tales from an Island
Peter Macnab
ISBN 0 946487 07 3 PB £8.99

The Supernatural Highlands
Francis Thompson
ISBN 0 946487 31 6 PB £8.99

GENEALOGY

Scottish Roots: step-by-step guide for ancestor hunters
Alwyn James
ISBN 1 84282 007 9 PB £9.99

SPORT

Over the Top with the Tartan Army
Andy McArthur
ISBN 0 946487 45 6 PB £7.99

Ski & Snowboard Scotland
Hilary Parke
ISBN 0 946487 35 9 PB £6.99

FICTION

The Road Dance
John MacKay
ISBN 1 84282 040 0 PB £6.99

Milk Treading
Nick Smith
ISBN 1 84282 037 0 PB £6.99

The Strange Case of RL Stevenson
Richard Woodhead
ISBN 0 946487 86 3 HB £16.99

But n Ben A-Go-Go
Matthew Fitt
ISBN 0 946487 82 0 HB £10.99
ISBN 1 84282 014 1 PB £6.99

Grave Robbers
Robin Mitchell
ISBN 0 946487 72 3 PB £7.99

The Bannockburn Years
William Scott
ISBN 0 946487 34 0 PB £7.95

The Great Melnikov
Hugh MacLachlan
ISBN 0 946487 42 1 PB £7.95

The Fundamentals of New Caledonia
David Nicol
ISBN 0 946487 93 6 HB £16.99

Heartland
John MacKay
ISBN 1 84282 059 1 PB £9.99

Driftnet
Lin Anderson
ISBN 1 84282 034 6 PB £9.99

Torch
Lin Anderson
ISBN 1 84282 042 7 PB £9.99

The Blue Moon Book
Anne Macleod
ISBN 1 84282 061 3 PB £9.99

The Glasgow Dragon
Des Dillon
ISBN 1 84282 056 7 PB £9.99

Six Black Candles [B format edition]
Des Dillon
ISBN 1 84282 053 2 PB £6.99

Me and Ma Gal [B format edition]
Des Dillon
ISBN 1 84282 054 0 PB £5.99

The Golden Menagerie
Allan Cameron
ISBN 1 84282 057 5 PB £9.99

POETRY

Drink the Green Fairy
Brian Whittingham
ISBN 1 84282 045 1 PB £8.99

The Ruba'iyat of Omar Khayyam, in Scots
Rab Wilson
ISBN 1 84282 046 X PB £8.99 (book)
ISBN 1 84282 070 2 £9.99 (audio CD)

Talking with Tongues
Brian Finch
ISBN 1 84282 006 0 PB £8.99

Kate o Shanter's Tale and other poems
Matthew Fitt
ISBN 1 84282 028 1 PB £6.99 (book)
ISBN 1 84282 043 5 £9.99 (audio CD)

Bad Ass Raindrop
Kokumo Rocks
ISBN 1 84282 018 4 PB £6.99

Madame Fi Fi's Farewell and other poems
Gerry Cambridge
ISBN 1 84282 005 2 PB £8.99

Scots Poems to be Read Aloud
Introduced by Stuart McHardy
ISBN 0 946487 81 2 PB £5.00

Picking Brambles and other poems
Des Dillon
ISBN 1 84282 021 4 PB £6.99

Sex, Death & Football
Alistair Findlay
ISBN 1 84282 022 2 PB £6.99

Tartan & Turban
Bashabi Fraser
ISBN 1 84282 044 3 PB £8.99

Immortal Memories: A Compilation of Toasts to the Memory of Burns as delivered at Burns Suppers, 1801-2001
John Cairney
ISBN 1 84282 009 5 HB £20.00

Poems to be Read Aloud
Introduced by Tom Atkinson
ISBN 0 946487 00 6 PB £5.00

Men and Beasts: wild men and tame animals
Valerie Gillies and Rebecca Marr
ISBN 0 946487 92 8 PB £15.00

Caledonian Cramboclink: the Poetry of
William Neill
ISBN 0 946487 53 7 PB £8.99

The Luath Burns Companion
John Cairney
ISBN 1 84282 000 1 PB £10.00

LANGUAGE

Luath Scots Language Learner [Book]
L Colin Wilson
ISBN 0 946487 91 X PB £9.99

Luath Scots Language Learner [Double Audio CD Set]
L Colin Wilson
ISBN 1 84282 026 5 CD £16.99

Luath Press Limited
committed to publishing well written books worth reading

LUATH PRESS takes its name from Robert Burns, whose little collie Luath (*Gael.,* swift or nimble) tripped up Jean Armour at a wedding and gave him the chance to speak to the woman who was to be his wife and the abiding love of his life. Burns called one of *The Twa Dogs* Luath after Cuchullin's hunting dog in *Ossian's Fingal.* Luath Press was established in 1981 in the heart of Burns country, and is now based a few steps up the road from Burns' first lodgings on Edinburgh's Royal Mile.
Luath offers you distinctive writing with a hint of unexpected pleasures.

Most bookshops in the UK, the US, Canada, Australia, New Zealand and parts of Europe either carry our books in stock or can order them for you. To order direct from us, please send a £sterling cheque, postal order, international money order or your credit card details (number, address of cardholder and expiry date) to us at the address below. Please add post and packing as follows: UK – £1.00 per delivery address; overseas surface mail – £2.50 per delivery address; overseas airmail – £3.50 for the first book to each delivery address, plus £1.00 for each additional book by airmail to the same address. If your order is a gift, we will happily enclose your card or message at no extra charge.

Luath Press Limited
543/2 Castlehill
The Royal Mile
Edinburgh EH1 2ND
Scotland
Telephone: 0131 225 4326 (24 hours)
Fax: 0131 225 4324
email: gavin.macdougall@luath.co.uk
Website: www.luath.co.uk